The Jansen Otso
family

For the Hea
of all who
Read page
These

Red Earth Woman

3/17/09

Red Earth Woman

an autobiography on spiritual healing

♀

BY LINDA S. BOWLBY, M.D.
PSYCHIATRIST

Red Earth
PUBLISHING, INC.
Oklahoma City, Oklahoma

Copyright 2006 by Red Earth Publishing, Inc./www.redearthwoman.com

Printed in the United States of America.
ISBN 0-9779993-1-9
Library of Congress Catalog Number 2006927926
Cover and contents designed by Sandi Welch/www.2WDesignGroup.com
Cover photo of Antelope Canyon, located in northcentral Arizona, by Linda Bowlby.

CONTENTS

*Many names and locations have been changed
to protect the anonymity of those concerned.*

INTRODUCTION

IN THE CHOCTAW LANGUAGE, "Okla Homa" means "Land of the Red People." Not only is Oklahoma the land of the red people, it is also the land of the red soil.

I was reared in Oklahoma, but because of its supposed "lack of culture," I rejected my home state. However, after years of traversing my journey in various mental and geographic states, I have come to know that my roots lie deep within Oklahoma's soil.

As I drive through the Oklahoma countryside at planting time, I see rich red plowed fields, and the earth's scent fills my nostrils. When I dig in Oklahoma's soil, I find layers of red clay alternating with loam and, on the sloping hills, I see outcroppings of red sandstone. My soul resonates with Oklahoma's red earth.

Many native cultures speak of "Mother Earth" and Her sacred birthings. The ancient Pueblo people's kivas were places of worship in which they descended into underground structures, as if they were descending into the womb of Mother Earth.

Women and the earth have long been equated. The soil of Oklahoma speaks to my soul, and I am her daughter. I am a "Red Earth Woman." This is the story of my spiritual journey.

CHAPTER ONE

My Childhood Haven

♀

ON A MAY MORNING, I walk onto my front porch and look west over the tree-covered rolling hills of Oklahoma. Now in my fifties, I am at peace, but peace was hard won.

I live on my 144-acre farm, thirty miles east of Oklahoma City and a mile past Hogback Road. You can't get more country than that. With my own hammer, I built my home one nail, board, and stone at a time. Its outer walls are of red cedar and gray Oklahoma limestone. The roof is corrugated metal, and inside the ceiling is knotted pine. Light fills the rooms through south and west windows. I live "off-the-grid," because the gatekeeper of the building codes is the electric company and, in my usual renegade fashion, I refuse to allow anyone residing in downtown Oklahoma City the right to dictate how my home is built.

My troop of dogs follow me as I walk from the porch to the barn and on to the chicken house. After one of my rural clinics, Ben, a frisky black Labrador, came to me as a stray. Louise and Beth were abandoned and found their way to my farm. Louise is a tan pit bull mix and, as we walk together, she enjoys her favorite sport and clamps her mouth around the tail of my big shirt.

Beth is black, with white markings. Of unknown birth origins, Beth arrived with a wounded and battered spirit. We have a special bond. We came from the same place.

At the chicken pen, only I enter. My dogs like the taste of chicken. I feed and water Pete and my four hens. Pete heralds each new day, and I relish his morning bugle calls. I gather the eggs and compliment the hens on their labors. My chicken pen is surrounded by rose bushes and, on my return to the house, I enjoy the scent of roses wafted by the summer breeze.

My life and torment were a riddle to me until my forties, when I began to remember. In my search for happiness and my life's meaning, I traversed much education and many relationships. I was sure the answers lay outside of myself in learning and with the educated. They, those nameless, faceless dictators of society, told me it was so, but they were wrong, as they were about so many things. I went to college and medical school, followed by a residency and practice in pathology. Years later, I entered a second residency in psychiatry, in which I now practice. I see patients in my city office, but each evening, I return alone to the solace of my farm, where I synchronize my life with the ebb and flow of the earth.

I walk back to the porch and open the screen door. At its familiar creak, I smile. The front porch door of my grandmother Ollie's house had the same sound. In childhood, my grandmother was my only safe person, and her spirit continues to comfort me. As a child, I loved visiting my grandmother's Arkansas farm. Unlike my parents, Grandmother Ollie demanded nothing. She didn't criticize, scold, or punish. In her house, I could just be in my uninhibited silence, for I rarely spoke.

A visit to my grandmother was a treat reserved for family occasions and holidays. On such trips, my parents, brother, John Paul, and I traveled the winding roads through the scenic Ozark mountains. On arriving at grandmother's, we would drive into her front yard accompanied by a rolling dust fog from the dirt country road. Grandmother lived in a two-story tin-roofed, white frame home, and her yard always contained an odd assortment of old coupes, which I suspect were primarily of Ford and Chevrolet derivation. However, as a child, I was oblivious to such details. It was the 1950s. All I knew was they were old, dirty, rusty, and smelled bad.

On our arrival, grandmother would step out on her front porch with open arms and a big smile. On grandmother's long front porch sat glistening Arkansas quartz, cane-bottom chairs, and, during the summer, large pots of angel-winged begonias with drooping pink blossoms. The porch was also frequented by a motley collection of dogs. After grandmother hugged and planted a big kiss on everyone, we followed her from the porch through the squeaky screen door and entered the living room. As my parents followed her on into the kitchen, I would tarry in the living room and reacquaint myself with this beloved room's familiar objects. To the left of the door was a wall-mounted, wooden telephone with a speaker horn and a crank with which my grandmother rang "Central" to speak to the operator. Grandmother addressed the operator by name and often asked for her connection by names such as Gertrude, Vennie, or Clyde down the road. The living room was occupied by a rocker, old chairs and couches covered with blankets, a secretary desk, a pot-bellied wood stove, and stacks of family photos. On the wall hung a picture of a moose serenely standing in a mountain lake, drinking water at dawn. The floor was covered by linoleum, which was usually gritty from tracked in dirt.

After thoroughly surveying the living room, I would join the grown-ups in the kitchen and quietly listen as they discussed the most recent family news.

After catching up on the news, I would wonder off to inspect the house for new treasures. Since my father's youth, the house had expanded with additions. This jumbled hodge-podge of a home was my sanctuary and, on my visits, I explored its every nook and cranny. One closed-in side-porch off the kitchen had a bed with noisy springs. The second "side-room" had sprouted from the other side of the kitchen. It contained stacks of boxes from "auction sales" and a sink where we cleaned fish. This side-room led to the basement where there was a musty smell, shelves filled with grandmother's garden-grown canned goods, a shower, and a wringer washer.

The latter side-room also led to the back door, through which, for necessities, one headed downhill, through the chicken-yard, and behind the chicken-house to the outhouse. When nature called, I gingerly sat bare bottomed on the stickery wooden outhouse seat and watched the chickens scratch and peck for bugs and worms, for the outhouse door had long been absent. After completing my task, rough sheets of old Montgomery Ward catalogs served for wiping.

In the house, my favorite room was the "upstairs," where I spent much time alone. The upstairs was one large room extending the length of the house. My father and his three brothers had slept there as children. This room was like a barrack and contained a row of beds and book shelves filled with Uncle Clay's old law books. On one wall hung his law school graduation picture. To that date, Uncle Clay was the most educated family member. (*I know grandmother would be pleased that I became a physician. She liked helping people and was often called on by neighbors and friends to tend the sick.*) This upstairs room also contained a roll top desk with lots of drawers, which I frequently investigated for new treasures. My fantasies whisked me away as I explored this room filled with boxes and trunks containing mounds of old clothes and other purchases from auctions. My grandparents loved a good sale.

Even though my grandfather also resided in the home, it was always grandmother's house to me. My Grandfather Kit, named after Kit Carson, was quiet and sullen, and I gave him a wide berth. By his own claim, he was "Scotch-Irish" and had a hot temper and little patience for children. My father told the story of my grandfather getting so mad he hit a cow between the eyes with a two-by-four and killed it. I remember thinking that was an awfully expensive fit, because my grandparents' income came from the sale of cattle. My father also said that when he was a boy my grandfather would get mad and beat him and his brothers.

In the upstairs, the feather bed with the high headboard was my favorite spot in the room. I loved to sink into its softness and listen to the rain on the tin roof or read a book by the dangling light bulb overhead. On sunny mornings, I snuggled in my fluffy nest and listened to the chirping birds.

When grandmother's house was occupied by large family gatherings, I often rose before everyone else and attempted to creep down the squeaking narrow wooden staircase without awakening anyone. As I walked into the kitchen, the floor boards of the old house creaked and, in the morning through the kitchen windows, the rising sun greeted me. Sometimes my grandmother would already be up, and the kitchen would be filled with the aroma of frying bacon. I enjoyed my time alone with grandmother or, if she was still sleeping, I indulged myself in the uninterrupted morning sounds of the crowing roosters.

During the summers, I was allowed the treat of spending a few weeks alone with grandmother. On those long lazy hot days, I relished going fishing with her. For such occasions, my grandmother wore an old straw hat, a dress held together with safety pins, and shoes broken down in the heels. Before walking to one of the farm's ponds, grandmother and I took a coffee can to her garden, where she put her foot to the shovel, turning over large clods of black dirt containing grubs and fat juicy earthworms. With trepidation, I helped her gather the slimy critters and, with a full bait can, we headed toward the pond.

As we sat on the pond bank quietly fishing, I savored my grandmother's presence. We fished with cane poles, patiently watched our red and white bobbers on the waves, and waited for them to disappear, our cue for a fish. Our vigilance was usually rewarded with the excitement of landing a bass, sun perch, or catfish. After fatigue and sunburns had set in, I'd follow grandmother home along the well-trodden cow paths.

On returning to the house, we cleaned our catch by dispensing of heads, innards, and scales at the side-room sink. Then my grandmother fried our catch for supper. In the twilight, we ate at the kitchen table and listened to the old clock ticking on the wall and the chickens scratching and cackling outside the kitchen window. Sometimes my grandfather joined us, but often he ate later because when we ate, he was still in the barn doing his chores. When he did eat with us, our silent reverie, except for his slurping, remained uninterrupted, for grandfather rarely made conversation. After supper, I helped grandmother clear the table, wash, and dry the dishes.

A few times I ventured to the barn and watched grandfather milk the cows by hand. As he squeezed and pulled the cow's tits, the milk sprayed into a metal bucket. After milking, he carried the brimming bucket to the house for grandmother to strain and separate the milk. Later, she would churn the creamy layer into fluffy mounds of butter.

During my summer visits, grandmother and I would make trips to town for shopping. Before departing, grandmother donned a hat, for she had a hat for all occasions. Then, we climbed into one of her old cars. Our drive would take us by Aunt Vennie's house and the country school my father had attended. In town, we made our rounds about the square and, as I followed grandmother, I was introduced to everyone she met.

On Sundays, after I dressed, I delighted in watching grandmother's ritual as she prepared for church. On went her thick nylons with garters rolled below her knees. Then she jammed her feet into her sturdy black thick-heeled shoes. Grandmother's feet were always so swollen that I was amazed she could get her shoes on. Then she powdered profusely and struggled to pull her "Sunday dress" over her head. Next, she went to the dresser and searched through a jumble of objects to retrieve a brooch to prevent her dress from gaping in front. Next she haphazardly piled her cottony white hair on top of her head with the aid of combs and silver bobby pins. On this stack, she plopped her Sunday hat.

At church, I listened to the sermon and squirmed on the hard pews. As I sat by grandmother, I loved smelling her powder and hearing her sing those wonderful old hymns. As she sang, grandmother's voice rang out in its country twang, and I was proud to be her granddaughter.

After church services, we piled back into the old car and headed off down those bumpy dirt roads for Sunday dinner with the relatives. After dinner, the adults retired to the cane chairs and rockers on the porch. Those ancient relations had wonderful plants around their porches. I enjoyed lolling on the edge of the porch near the plants and listening to the grown-ups talk. The women talked of their gardening, canning, and sewing, and everyone swapped stories about relatives and times long past. In my child's mind, I tried to make sense of how I was related to these people, but I could never quite figure out our connection.

Other summer entertainments at grandmother's included the carnival's annual visit, and each year grandmother took me. As the calliope music played, I followed her as she wound her way through the crowd greeting everyone she knew. Now, I realize what an effort it was for her to walk through that dusty field on her swollen legs, but she never once complained. Grandmother and I always purchased cotton candy and, as we ate, I would throw a few balls at various objects in hopes of winning a doll or stuffed animal. As we departed the dusty field, grandmother usually came away with a gaudy piece of carnival glass and I with a colorfully beaded bracelet or necklace strung on an elastic cord, on which the beads broke like Christmas bulbs.

On hot humid days, grandmother took me swimming in the creek. There, I joined other children, often distant cousins, as we carefully waded barefoot over the rocky creek bed. An occasional brave soul grabbed a vine, swung out over the water, and jumped in. I was never that soul.

Some days I accompanied grandmother to the old country school where she joined other women for a "quilting bee." The ladies gathered around the quilt which was stretched tightly on a wooden frame. In the light streaming from the school windows, they talked and sewed. In the summer, open doors and windows allowed the breezes to waft through the room. On occasion, I was privileged to visit a winter quilting bee. After the fire was stoked, the potbellied stove kept the one-room building from hot to comfortable, depending on the amount of wood it contained. Whatever the temperature, I do not recall the working women ever complaining.

In that old country school, I played and listened with pleasure to the chatter of the quilting women. They were simple country women who grew gardens, canned, raised chickens, children, and grandchildren, and saved colorful bits of fabric for quilting. Frequently the quilts were being made for needy families, fire victims, or for a raffle to raise money for the school.

On winter evenings around my grandmother's wood stove, I watched her tear worn-out clothes into strips and pieces for quilting. Sometimes one of my outgrown dresses or pairs of pajamas wound up in those quilts. When this happened, I was pleased. Because, with all that work and beauty, quilts were very special. With remnants of my clothes in the quilt, that meant I must be special too.

Some evenings, I sat by grandmother in the roomy living room rocker as she read to me from a big book of Bible stories. From long use, the book's binding was unraveling and pages were loose, but that book was a treasure to me, because grandmother made those stories come alive. I listened enthralled. I knew grandmother believed in God and the Bible, so I figured God must exist, because my grandmother was a good person, and I trusted her.

My grandmother was always cooking, canning, and puttering in her kitchen, and her enamel gas stove was often laden with bubbling pots. The stove was flanked by two Hoosiers. The kitchen also contained a large wooden table haphazardly surrounded by an odd collection of ancient wooden dining room chairs. The kitchen was also furnished with two oak buffets covered by a jumbled and incongruous assortment of objects and a pie safe containing chipped dishes and Depression glassware. In the middle of the kitchen was a free-standing sink surrounded by a cloth curtain.

Some of my fondest memories occurred in that kitchen.

On the mornings of large family gatherings, my grandmother heaped the table with platters of bacon, fried eggs, biscuits, gravy, and homemade butter and jams. At supper, grandmother again loaded the table with fried chicken, fish, or steak and mounds of mashed potatoes, gravy, homemade bread, and canned pickles and relishes. The meal was always concluded with freshly baked pies and cakes. After supper and the women and children had washed, dried, and put away the dishes, everyone gathered around the kitchen table and told stories and played games. Those present usually included my parents and my brother, who was three years younger than me and a royal pain. Much to my despair, he enjoyed hitting me, and I frequently wore his bruises. Also present at those gatherings was an odd assortment of my father's brothers and their wives and children. Uncle Fred and his wife, Aunt Eva, frequently came from their home in Kansas City. They had no children. Sometimes Uncle Clay and his wife, Aunt Rosie, and their two children, Clay Robert and Mary Sue, journeyed from Tennessee. On a rare occasion, Uncle Bill and his wife, Aunt Jewell, and their two boys, Jerry and Jessie, came from California. Occasionally, there would be an extra great uncle or two.

Uncle Fred and Aunt Eva were my favorites. They had a nice home in Kansas City which was furnished in good taste. Because they had no children, Uncle Fred and Aunt Eva always enjoyed spending time with us, the nieces and nephews. Uncle Fred frequently joked and kidded with us, and Aunt Eva was gentle, kind, and always smelled good. Aunt Eva was a lady, and I wanted to be like her.

Uncle Clay was quiet and scholarly. Aunt Rosie talked incessantly, bragging on her two children. Clay Robert and Mary Sue were spoiled brats. To hear Aunt Rosie talk, I always had the impression that Oak Ridge, Tennessee, where they lived, must be the intellectual capital of the world. She was always telling of her children's advanced educational experiences and achievements.

Aunt Rosie, to hear my parents tell it, was a dried-up old maid school teacher who finally hooked a husband and had children. From my viewpoint, Clay Robert threw constant fits and never did what he was told, and Mary Sue thought she was trying out for a princess role. They disgusted me.

Uncle Bill, who was rarely present, was considered the black sheep of the family, but I was never quite sure why. There were vague family rumors that he drank too much. I always had the impression Aunt Jewell was considered a bit of a trollop, but I liked them and their sons.

After dinner, those gathered about the kitchen table loved to match wits in games of cards or dominoes, and I was always in the thick of it. By a year or two, I was the oldest child, and my brother and cousins couldn't sit still and keep quiet long enough to play with the grown-ups. Though relatively uneducated, my family held intelligence in high esteem and enjoyed games of strategy. I relished sparring with the grown-ups and, much to my glee, I occasionally won.

If it was summer, croquet was included in the family's after meal sport. The front porch housed racks of mallets and balls, and the wickets were in place on the croquet field, grandmother's all-purpose front yard. Croquet was also a game of skill and strategy and, again, I would be there taking my turn.

My grandfather was always up for a game of any kind, and he liked to win. During these family gatherings, grandfather was chided for his unsportsmanlike conduct, and my father and uncles made him follow the rules. On my solo visits, under the watchful eye of grandmother, grandfather and I engaged on the game field, and he played for blood, but grandmother made him follow the rules. When I on occasion won, he got mad and sulked, but I still delighted in winning.

Whether it was a solitary or family visit to grandmother's, the time came all too soon to leave my sanctuary and return home to my parents' Oklahoma farm, where life went on in its labored, plodding fashion.

♀ ♀ ♀

I awake from my reverie. On entering the house, I collect my sewing box and scraps of quilting fabric and head to the front porch rocker. From my grandmother, I inherited a love for quilting and, like her, I hand stitch quilt blocks. In quilting, I take colored pieces of assorted fabric and make a new whole. The quilt I am working on now combines the pieces from a dress I wore several winters ago, with the pieces left from the curtains I made for a cabin in Alaska, and the pieces left from a dress I made for my daughter, Sarah. As I quilt, I bring together the fabrics of my life. Sometimes strange colors, shapes, and sizes of fabric find their way into my quilt but, with reflection and time, I see they form a beautiful pattern that tells my life's story.

CHAPTER TWO

In My Parents' Home

♀

As I STITCH QUILT BLOCKS from the various fabrics of my life, I reflect on my childhood.

In my parents' home, we played the family games of cards, dominoes, and croquet. We matched wits, and I honed my skills. The joviality and banter were temporary. Criticism was the norm.

By visitors, we were viewed as a happy family. On the surface, my father was handsome, charming, flirtatious, and the life of the party. My mother was industrious and organized, and she kept everyone supplied with food and beverages. Beneath the banter and camaraderie, out of the sight of company, was a tension that I knew all too well. Anger lived in every corner of our home. There was no margin for error in my family's unwritten and often unspoken rules. I tried to do what I thought was required, but I was doomed to failure. My perceived disobedience brought swift and harsh reprisal. For minute or invisible infractions, I often knew the sound of my mother's angry voice and felt a stick, flyswatter, or first available object on my bare skin. As we circled, with her holding onto me with one hand

and hitting me with the other, I cried, and she screamed, "Don't you cry, or I'll give you something to cry about." For more severe punishment, there was my father and his dreaded belt. I never "talked back." I worked hard at being "good," but I always fell short of my parents' benchmark. I lived in fear, like a deer in headlights.

Photographs taken of me throughout my childhood show a withdrawn, brooding, self-conscious child, with downcast eyes. My world was very serious.

For a brief moment, at age four, I was given a glimpse of another world. My mother enrolled me in ballet classes. Though very shy, I was coaxed to dance as a butterfly, fluttering my wings with other little girls as we circled under our mothers' watchful eyes. Soon mother became disenchanted with my dancing career and the twelve-mile drive to Morton. Besides, she had sick lambs to tend.

To escape my reality, at six or seven I planned to build my own home. While my parents were building a barn, I hammered nails through a board into the dirt. All the while and with great anticipation, I visualized the white lace curtains covering the window over my kitchen sink. From ages seven through ten, I spent hours by the creek, which was barely within shouting distance of my parents' house. From an arbor of sticks, I made my home, where I brought my dishes and imaginary family. Silently, I caught crawdads in the creek, played, and was content. Other times, I took solitary walks in the fields on my parents' or neighbors' farms. Out on the land, I felt free and peaceful.

From an early age, my brother and I were part of the labor force. Being the youngest and male, my mother favored John

Paul and he usually did more playing than work. She and I had to take up his slack.

In summers, my mother, brother, and I worked in the garden, picking green beans, peas, corn, or whatever needed gathering. While my mother canned or prepared food for freezing, I helped shell peas, snap green beans, shuck corn, cut up apples or pears or peaches, or remove stems from strawberries. I felt hot, sweaty, dirty, and ugly. I longed to be clean, feel pretty, and go play.

Year-round, there was housecleaning and hanging clothes on the clothesline, even with numb fingers in freezing weather. These activities were followed by folding or sprinkling and ironing clothes. My mother and I shared in the family ironing. Often in anger, I slammed that iron down on my father's and brother's clothes, for I inwardly rebelled against the unwritten rule that because they were "men" they were entitled to have their laundry done for them.

Depending on our age and what animals my parents were raising, my brother and I had "outdoor" chores. From about ages eight to ten, my most dreaded chore was slopping the hogs. Several times a week, with my arm feeling like it was pulling out of its socket, I carried a five-gallon bucket of slop from the house to the hog pen. As I walked the interminable distance, the slop often sloshed over the sides of the bucket and onto me. I silently cringed with the indignity of that rotting waste on my body. I despised those squealing, nasty, foul-smelling hogs.

Once, I had an egg-sized groin abscess, but I still had to slop those hogs. When the pain became so severe I couldn't walk, I was taken into town to Dr. Carter. The abscess was lanced and drained. I was grudgingly given a few days without chores, but there was no sympathy or concern. I now know an abscess in a young girl's groin is a red flag for any physician who is alert to the signs of sexual abuse.

In all weather, including ice and snow, I brought in the cows for evening milking. Cautiously attempting to avoid the manure piles, I followed the cow paths over the hill to the distant pastures. After locating the cows, I gathered them and herded them into the barn. I was not particularly fond of cows, but often I enjoyed my walk and its solitude, especially if I was able to circumvent the cow piles. I became upset when I stepped in one, especially when I was barefoot.

MY APPEARANCE

Because of my appearance, I felt like a country hayseed. Except when Aunt Eva was visiting, my hair received only my inept care. My mother was busy with the milking, morning and evening, while my father worked nights at a factory in Morton. My clothes were ill fitting and usually made by my mother. When I was in my preteens and learning to sew in 4-H, mother turned my clothing construction over to me. I looked like I felt—sad.

Each fall, when the Penney's and Montgomery Ward catalogs arrived in the mail, I spent hours pouring over the pages and selecting my fall wardrobe. Of course, the order was never placed, and the mail contained no package for me.

The only time I received "store bought" clothes was at Christmas and my birthday, but my mother's taste ill-suited me. Except for shoes, the first time I recall going into a store to purchase clothing for myself was when I was fifteen. One of my 4-H projects was to show a heifer at the county fair. I disliked the whole notion of interacting with a cow, but the prize money lured me to train and groom the animal. After the deed was done and resulted in a blue ribbon, I proudly marched to Penney's with the prize money and purchased a matching brown skirt and blouse.

In my limited wardrobe, I walked one-fourth mile to catch the bus on every school day for twelve years. There was never a warm car ride to the end of the lane in cold weather. My brother and I were the first to get on in the morning, so we had to ride the whole route. Julie, a year younger than I, moved to our town when I was in the seventh grade, and she rode my bus. Each morning, a smiling Julie would get on with her two older cousins, Larry and Jeff, and each day, I enviously viewed what she wore and checked to see if it was new. Julie had a seemingly endless array of skirt and sweater sets, of which I had none. I always sat some distance behind Julie. Even though I thought she had a big nose and wasn't that pretty, Julie exuded confidence and was very popular.

SCHOOL

I began the first grade at age five. I was terrified. Mrs. Sapp, a huge towering woman with tightly permed curls, had no business teaching small children. The first graders would have been better served if she had taught auto mechanics. Her sister, Miss Lane, taught second grade, and her other sister, Mrs. Roberts, taught third. I was doomed. Mrs. Jackson, a woman of similar ilk as the dreaded three sisters, taught fourth grade. There was some small relief by the fifth grade. By the seventh and eight grades, I was used to making C's, and for some unknown reason, possibly hormones, I often talked out loud in those grades and was required to write extra themes. Finally, Mr. Hampton, my history teacher, confronted me and said, "If you wanted to, you could make straight A's." He made me so mad, I showed him and made the highest score in the class on his next exam, then promptly returned to making C's.

Jeannie was my best friend in grade school. My parents played cards with Jeannie's parents, so we frequently visited each other's homes, and occasionally Jeannie and I were given the treat of spending the night together. Jeannie lived on Grand Lake and had access to a dock and her parents' boat, so we spent many blissful hours fishing and talking.

Before high school, my mother abruptly severed my relationship with Jeannie. Mother had concluded that Jeannie's mother, Virginia, was having affairs, possibly with my father, and that Jeannie was going to be "wild." Since I was to remain a virgin at all costs, I was no longer allowed to associate with my friend. Shortly thereafter, Jeannie moved away. I was desolate.

Throughout grade school and high school, I was the youngest in my class of twenty-five. By my freshman year, my nervous system began to catch up with the rest of my classmates. I realized, with some effort, I could indeed make all A's, and that became my only defense, because the "town girls" were my nemesis. Eileen, the principal's daughter, and Bonnie, the Baptist minister's daughter, were in my class and were the social hub of the high school. I was from the country and a Methodist, both the kiss of death in our small town of Fairfield, Oklahoma, population 625. However, when it came to tests, I could beat Eileen and Bonnie going and coming, which gave me some small comfort.

OUR HOME

Not only did I feel inferior for being from the country, being a Methodist, and wearing homemade clothes, I was embarrassed by my parents' house.

Before school started each year, my mother would take my brother and me to buy us each a new pair of school shoes. Our shoes became too small or worn out by spring so, much to our delight, we went barefoot in the summers. Before school started my second grade year, we visited Uncle Fred and Aunt Eva in Kansas City and bought shiny new shoes. In the first week of school, I begged my mother to let me wear my new shoes to school, but she said, "No, wear your old ones. They still have some good left in them." While I was at school, our house burnt to the ground. My new shoes and my only companions, my dolls, were gone. That night as I lay in a neighbor's bed, I was in shock, but I also felt a glimmer of hope. "Maybe our new home and life would be wonderful?" Such were the dreams of a sad and lonely child.

For several years, we lived in a makeshift arrangement of a small trailer, with an equally small built-on living room and bedroom. The latter housed a set of crudely welded steel-framed bunk beds. Since my brother was the youngest, he got the bottom bunk. While in that house, we got our first black and white television, which, along with books, brought me some exposure and escape to the outside world. Ed Sullivan, Dinah Shore, Perry Como, and the Hit Parade depicted the life I wanted to live, beautiful and carefree.

About six years after the fire, Uncle Fred came to stay with us. He was a master homebuilder. Aided by my mother, who worked harder than most men, Uncle Fred built our new house, and I spent long hours watching him work and enjoying his kind companionship. Our new house was simple but nice. The furnishings were crude and artless.

Even though she was a Baptist, Janice Gorman befriended me. I suspect it was out of pity. I was occasionally invited to Janice's home. I always wanted to have a home and mother like Janice's. Her mother was a housewife and cooked wonderful meals, and there was a homey atmosphere in her kitchen. Mrs. Gorman had nice things and kept her house clean. Janice had a lovely room, with floral wallpaper, pretty furniture, frilly curtains, and a bedspread. Mrs. Gorman bought Janice nice clothes, and they both had their hair done at the beauty shop. I never invited Janice to my house. I think she understood.

Besides Janice's house, visits to Uncle Fred and Aunt Eva's home in Kansas City were my only exposure to any shred of elegance. Aunt Eva had pretty things and artfully decorated her home. I felt as if I were in the lap of luxury in her guest bedroom, where I slept on a white, wrought-iron framed bed and snuggled under a white crocheted bedspread.

CHURCH

Besides school and occasional visits with relatives, church was my only relief from country life. On Sundays, I dressed in my awkward best. As a small child, I daydreamed or attempted to listen to sermons that made no sense except to scare me about hell and the devil. If I squirmed on the hard seats or made sounds, my mother pinched me or pulled my hair. With more severe misconduct, she spanked me after the service. I was never quite sure why we went to church. I never felt better afterward.

In grade school, the main benefit to church was summer Bible school, with its singing, crafts, cookies, Kool-Aid, and Mrs. Love. Mrs. Love played the piano and supervised Bible school, and her name described her. In our small town, she was the gentlest, kindest person I knew, and I was comforted knowing someone like Mrs. Love existed.

Once each summer, the church also had an "Ice Cream Social." The women prepared the various ice creams, which often contained fresh fruit, especially strawberries, blackberries, and peaches, and the men provided the muscle to crank the handles of the ice cream mixers, as the children played and waited with anticipation. I silently stood watching from the sidelines. After the ice cream "set," even though I was told to "watch my figure," I stood in line with my bowl and sampled each flavor, sometimes twice.

For a week, in my preteens, I nightly attended a revival. I desperately wanted God to love and care for me, so of course I went down for the call to be saved. I knelt, cried, prayed, and hoped my life would be better. It wasn't.

As I grew older, my required church attendance became even more upsetting. Though I no longer had to sit with my mother, I was a year younger than the other three teenage girls in the church and not included in their group. Sandy was the ringleader and vicious. Beckie and Nancy went along with her, and I was often the subject of their cruel gossip and spiteful looks.

By high school, I didn't believe much in the Methodists or Baptists, because they sure as heck didn't practice what they preached. At school, the kids from the Church of Christ weren't much better. My father hated the Catholics, even though I doubt if he ever knew one. Religions outside of Christianity were out of my realm of consciousness. I was pretty lost when it came to God.

FUN TIMES

There were pleasant and relaxing times in my childhood, but I was always reserved and hesitant in any situation.

I enjoyed our horses. As a young child, I rode Penny, a gentle old mare who plodded along oblivious to the antics occurring on her back. John Paul and I often rode double, and occasionally there would be an added cousin or visiting child of my parents' friends. As I grew older, I rode Buck, Penny's son, whom Penny had birthed at age twenty. Her late motherhood had earned Penny a write-up in the local newspaper. On Buck, I rode with the wind, feeling free and strong, but I had a problem getting Buck stopped. Often, as he charged over the hills and through the pastures, the only thing that got his attention was a barbed wire fence. As he put on the brakes, I held on for dear life.

In the 1950s in rural Oklahoma, other simple pleasures included "Box Suppers" held in country schools, as contrasted to the school in Fairfield. In preparation as my mother and I carefully fried chicken, made deviled eggs, and baked pies or cakes, I felt the thrill of anticipation of the upcoming event. On the appointed evening, I donned my favorite dress in hopes of that special boy buying my box. Such sweet innocence.

Then came the bidding on my carefully wrapped box. I anxiously watched, as the appropriately prompted boy bid. Always, the older men joined in the fun, teased and taunted the desired courtship, raised the bid, and increased the revenue for the school fund.

After the bidding, the girls and women claimed their boxes and ate dinner with the man or boy with the winning bid. Under the watchful community eye, the boy and I awkwardly ate in this courtship ritual. Then in the fading evening light, there might be a shyly held hand or quickly stolen kiss, before each of us went home with our parents.

Other pleasures growing up included dancing. For years, my parents openly defied our Baptist-ruled town's dictum of "No Dancing" and scandalously spearheaded the weekly Saturday night dance at the Legion Hall. My brother and I regularly accompanied them to these dances so, from an early age, I danced the two-step, fox trot, bunny-hop, and waltz. To these events, the women brought all types of pies and cakes, which were served at "Intermission'" with coffee and Kool-Aid. Although it was against the rules, the men stole outside and took a nip now and then. There was rarely a boy my age in attendance. In my preteens and teens, as the fiddlers played and the couples circled the dance floor, I frequently was asked to dance by adult men who, unknown to me at the time, were sometimes in their cups. As we circled, they held me tight, and we bounced along to the music. I had a great time and had no idea this might be considered inappropriate for a girl my age.

Annual vacations were also a part of our family's recreation. Long before the vacation, my mother and I made ourselves new short and blouse sets, and mother made my brother and father new shirts. Obviously issuing from the country, we headed out to visit relatives in Texas, Kansas, Tennessee, or California. To look my best, I dieted before each trip, then felt fat during and after the trip because all family activities were punctuated with food. For the road, mother packed all types of sandwiches, chips, and cookies. Then came the relative's elaborate home cooked meals, and once or twice on each trip we had the expensive luxury of eating out at a Mexican, Chinese, or seafood restaurant.

No matter where we went, our trips were always accompanied by tension. My brother and I were constantly instructed to "be good, be quiet, and sit still," or my parents might become angry, especially my father. Easily angered, he swore and carried on and, when happy, he laughed, joked, and kidded. Everyone danced to my father's moods.

FIRST LOVE

My first two years of high school were much improved by my boyfriend, Henry. For the first time in my life, I felt happy and loved.

At school, Henry and I were constant companions. We held hands and stole an occasional kiss. We planned our love to last forever. Henry was from a large German farm family, and he wanted to get married, live on a farm, and raise six kids. My father had always told me if I wanted to get off the farm, I needed to go to college. I definitely wanted a life of refinement and beauty, so I wanted to go to college, live in a distant city, and lead a sophisticated life. I felt I would die if I lived Henry's dream, and I knew he couldn't live mine. Finally, with a heavy heart, I broke up with Henry.

Henry's love had been my warm buffer from school and my parents. My last two years of high school were torture. Henry fell in love with Julie. I watched in the school halls as Henry held Julie's hand and kissed and caressed her. I was in agony. Thank goodness she no longer rode the school bus. (*Later, Julie and Henry "had" to get married and went on to live on a farm and rear six children.*)

As Henry courted Julie, I pleaded with my parents to send me to the Arkansas work-program boarding school they had attended in high school. They refused. In my class, I was in a group of one, the smartest kid. I continued my solitary, silent march.

MY SENIOR YEAR

There was a brief intermission from my agony. As a reward for scholastic achievement, the summer before my senior year I attended a science camp on a college campus in Kalamazoo, Michigan. I was in the company of other students like myself. The boys actually liked and pursued me. For the first time in my life, I felt pretty and popular. However, I was ill prepared by my small rural high school for the camp's advanced mathematics and science classes.

I left for Kalamazoo with an hourglass figure. Though five feet five inches tall and 115 pounds, I felt fat and had dieted since early childhood. Because of his work schedule, my father only attended weekend family meals. During these meals he delivered variations on a series of sermons. One recurrent theme was on a woman's duty to her husband. In that series, I heard, "A woman is to look good, keep her figure, cook well, keep a clean house, be faithful, and please her husband sexually." My father further held if a woman did not do her "duty," her husband had the right to seek his comfort elsewhere.

At the science camp, to cope with the academic stress, I began to binge on huge quantities of candy bars and pastries. On a deep subconscious level, the binging and weight gain were also an escape from male attention and my mounting sexual attraction to a fellow student from Ohio, John Lovejoy. Along with the binging, I picked my skin to red sores and brutally cut my hair to short stubs.

After camp was over, I returned home with a significant weight gain. As I stepped off the bus, I was embarrassed for my parents to see me. Shortly after my return, my mother slapped me and accused me of being pregnant. Nothing could have been further from the truth.

My senior year was a tug-of-war over food between mother and me. Never before had I openly defied her. Until then, I had been the submissive daughter. Because of mother's rearing during the Depression and her fear of lack, she kept the home stocked with enormous quantities of food, especially baked goods and ice cream. Because of my weight gain, I was allowed to eat only my mealtime allotment, and my eating a dessert was frowned upon. The battle was on. The more my mother restricted and punished me for eating, the more I ate. She counted the number of cookies and slices of bread. She marked the level of ice cream in its containers. I ate from the bottom of the ice cream box and ignored her counting. With my burgeoning body, my wardrobe became nonexistent, and it was a trial to identify something I could wear to school.

Eventually, I was reduced to repeatedly wearing one garment, the only one that fit. Of course, I was incredibly depressed and physically miserable.

That fall, we had a home football game, and I was the band's head twirler. I felt fat and ugly and didn't want to prance to music in a short skirt. Besides, I had a date after the game with the school nerd, Buddy Krofton, and I was embarrassed to be seen with him.

I went to the bathroom and took a huge quantity of pills. I thought of taking more but decided, no, if that wouldn't do it, nothing would. I proceeded to tell my mother I was sick and went to bed. From a deep sleep, mother roused me and, against my protests, forced me to go to the game. I performed all evening in a drugged stupor and afterwards endured a hamburger with Buddy.

In the meantime, my mother went to the medicine cabinet for John Paul and found the pills missing. On arriving home that night, mother railed at me then drove me to the hospital in Morton. On a stretcher in the emergency room, I drifted in and out of consciousness. My classmate Bonnie and her twin brother, Ronnie, came to check on me. I wondered how they knew I was there and why they came? I didn't think they liked me.

Later, I was in a hospital bed, in a semi-conscious state. Hovering out of my body, my spirit looked on the scene as Dr. Carter told my parents it was too late to pump my stomach. My body had metabolized the pills. He didn't expect me to live. At that moment, I knew to the core of my being that it was not time for me to die, because God had work for me to do. For that brief instant I glimpsed the divinity of my being and inwardly smiled at the folly of the doctor and my parents, for they were not privy to God's plan. I was sixteen.

A day or two later, Dr. Carter came into my private room. He said he needed to examine me. He fondled my clitoris. I became aroused. The feeling disturbed me. I pretended to feel nothing. He persisted. At that time, I had no conscious idea of what a clitoris or sexual arousal were. During the doctor's "examination," my mother abruptly entered the room. He quickly removed his hand from beneath the sheet, briefly spoke to my mother, then left the room. My mother did not explain to me what had happened. I was bewildered.

On my hospital discharge and for the first time that I can remember, mother took me clothes shopping. She bought me the prettiest clothes I had ever worn—two Bobbie Brooks sweater and skirt sets. Wearing my new clothes, I felt like I might be able to fit in with the other girls.

I returned to school and endured. In the early 1960s in rural Oklahoma, no one had heard of teenage suicide or therapy. The food war with my mother continued through the winter.

My senior year was interrupted one day while sitting in Mr. Barker's biology class. Another teacher came to the classroom door and announced President Kennedy had been shot. We were stunned. The school crowded around our only television. Horrified, we heard the news. The Kennedys were royalty. How could this happen to them? Jackie in her pill box hats and tailored suits or regal eveningwear was our nation's model of elegance and grace, and President Kennedy was our hope for the future. The nation grieved. Then, life moved on.

In the spring, I began to feel less depressed. I "dieted" and lost some weight, and I allowed my hair to grow back into soft brown curls. I had continued in 4-H throughout high school, and my sewing project that spring was my senior banquet formal. After school, chores, and studies, I stayed up late each night sewing. The dress was floor-length, sleeveless, and of shell-pink brocade, with an embossed rose pattern. It was to be the most beautiful garment I had ever worn, and the vision of how I would look in it drove me to exhaustion. During this time, my parents traveled to Mexico with a group bus tour, leaving my brother and me at home alone. I began to feel sick, but as usual I ignored my symptoms and continued my late night vigils. After several days, I became so ill I told my 4-H sponsor, the woman who helped me with my sewing. That same day, she took me to my new doctor, Dr. Mary, located in Janson, a town forty miles away. When Dr. Mary saw the results of my blood tests, I was immediately hospitalized and given intravenous antibiotics.

While in my lovely hospital gown adorned with tomato soup from lunch, in walked Eileen with her husband Jack and his twin brother, Bob. When she was a junior, Eileen and Jack had one of those quick weddings, but she lost the baby. She and Jack alternated living with his or her parents. Jack and Bob were sophomores at Morton's junior college. A few weeks previously, Jack and Eileen had set up a double date with Bob and me. After the date, I was sure I had miserably failed the test and would never see Bob again. Lo and behold, here he was in my hospital room. I wanted to hide under the covers but, with great aplomb, I managed to carry on a conversation. I was pleased, puzzled, and relieved when they left. A few days later without apparent concern, my parents arrived and took me home.

To my surprise, after returning home, Bob called to check on me, and we began to date. He asked me to the ROTC Ball. I had been working on weekends cleaning houses, so I was able to buy a few clothes. For the ball, I wore a below-the-knee length white dress, with white gloves and heels. As was the custom, Bob gave me a corsage of orchids. As Bob introduced me in the receiving line to his commanding officers, I almost felt like a lady. A few weeks later, Bob escorted me to my senior banquet, and I proudly wore my pink formal, on which I had won runner-up to grand champion at the 4-H "style show." With the formal, I wore long white gloves, and heels dyed to match my dress. Since Fairfield was run by the Baptists, we were not allowed to have a prom. Nevertheless, I felt quite elegant and immensely enjoyed the evening.

Graduation arrived. I was valedictorian. My speech was on the beauty of a budding rose and its analogy to graduation and our personal unfolding. My speech horrified Mrs. Tripplett, the rotund high school accounting teacher. Mrs. Tripplett was in charge of the graduation ceremony, and she yearly distributed a collection of lengthy speeches from which that year's valedictorian was to select and memorize one. My audience was stunned and somewhat baffled by the brevity of my address. They hadn't had time to settle in for a good nap.

When I look at photographs of the senior banquet and graduation, I see a teenage girl who looks like an automaton. She had no clue to what lurked in her forgotten memory. She was going through the motions, doing what adolescent girls did in rural Oklahoma towns in 1964.

CHAPTER THREE

College and Vietnam

♀

AFTER HIGH SCHOOL GRADUATION, along with the Baptist minister's twins, I took a summer job waiting tables at a nearby posh lake resort. The resort guests were from walks of life about which I could only read or dream. With constant food exposure, I again began to binge and gain weight. I was miserable.

After work late one August night, Ronnie, Bonnie, and I went down to the dock and boarded the resort's motorized version of a Mississippi River paddleboat. While there, we talked, listened to music, danced, and felt deliciously sinful. The club bartender also accompanied us and mixed drinks. Never having consumed alcohol, I proceeded to drink several Harvey Wallbangers like fruit punch. The next thing I remember, I had jumped overboard into the inviting water below. I wanted the water to engulf me and take me away.

Ronnie, Bonnie, and others hauled me out, dried me off, and took me home. That was the end of my waitressing career, and the rest of the summer was spent with my parents on the farm and in the fields.

This was my second suicide attempt in a year. My parents did not discuss it with me. There was no psychiatrist, therapy, or help for the deep depression that rocked my soul.

That summer, Bob worked out of state. On his return, along with Jack and Eileen, he enrolled at Oklahoma State University, in Stillwater, Oklahoma, more than a hundred miles from Fairfield. I was extremely disappointed when, because of finances, my parents forced me to stay home and attend Morton's junior college.

Nothing had changed between my mother and me except that in the preceding year she had started classes in the same college. In stony silence, we daily rode together to and from school. We were even in the same algebra and chemistry classes. I had always excelled in those subjects. Frequently being the subject of my mother's wrath, I had never felt she liked me, let alone loved me, so I relished my superiority over her in the classroom.

As the year wore on and much to my science and mathematics teachers' chagrin, I changed my major from science to philosophy and art history. After a culturally deprived rural environment, I hungered for the arts and, through this interest, I met JoNell, my first close friend since Jeannie. JoNell grew up in Morton, in a home filled with the sounds of classical music and shelves burgeoning with art books. Her mother was a music teacher and her father an artist. JoNell was an art major and had led a sheltered and genteel life. Like a starving puppy, I followed her around in awe as she shared her home, knowledge, and art books.

Besides JoNell, another highlight of my freshman year was my first observance of professional dancers. The college hosted Martha Graham's ex-husband's dance troupe. I was mesmerized by their artistic form, poetic movement, and emotional intensity. I later discovered, although only at the movies or on television, Joan Fontaine and Rudolf Nureyez. I longed to move my body with such grace.

My obsession with food and compulsion to binge were unrelenting. I worked part-time jobs at the college and city libraries. Using all the money I earned, I bought countless candy bars and pastries from the school vending machines and local convenience stores. I isolated myself and ate. My depression grew worse. Food was my misery's only anesthesia. For days and weeks on end, I wore one brown skirt, with two to three variations in blouses. The skirt's waistband constricted me, and my blouses gaped. In 1965, our clothes were without elastic waistbands or stretchy fabrics. I existed. I made A's in school. I lived in my mind, but my mind was a morose place to be. Finally, my freshman year of college ended.

I worked in Morton's library that summer and continued to date Bob, who had completed his junior year at Oklahoma State. During the previous school year, we had written letters and saw each other on an occasional weekend. However, because I looked and felt so awful, I dreaded his visits and, actually, I wasn't sure if Bob and I were a good fit. I thought about breaking up with him but didn't want to hurt his feelings.

I faced another year at home with my mother and the junior college. In those days, "good girls" didn't have sex before marriage. Bob and I wanted to have sex, so I decided the only solution was to get married. Then we could have sex, I could get away from home and my mother, and Bob's feelings would remain intact. I proposed. Bob accepted.

I wanted to go to the justice of the peace for the ceremony and avoid the family scene. My mother cried and carried on. Finally, with anger and disgust, I gave in to her, but I stipulated she had to do all of the work, because I wanted nothing to do with the arrangements, except for my dress.

I made a matronly tailored double-breasted white wool wedding dress styled after Jackie, minus the hat. I cut my hair, squeezed my pimples, and binged the night before our wedding and, of course, on my wedding day, I felt fat and ugly. However, the day had a moment of levity. My mother procured the minister. He was drunk. While kneeling for our vows, Bob and I laughed so hard at his garbled speech we almost rolled down the aisle. I figured it served my mother right for putting me through the family charade.

Bob and I were too poor for a honeymoon or a car so, after the ceremony, we were driven to our new apartment in Stillwater. There was no trousseau lovingly selected by my mother. For my wedding night, I made my robe of olive green cotton, with a matching print gown. I shudder to remember how unflattering they were. Their only saving grace was their necklines revealing my ample bosom. I felt like a beached whale, and Bob did nothing to relieve my self-consciousness.

Our first week of married life was followed by the commencement of fall classes. Since we were without transportation, we lived within walking distance of the campus. Our only source of income was school loans and money from Bob's parents. Bob and I were as happy as we knew how to be. Unfortunately, neither of us had an acquaintance with that emotion.

To compound my misery, we lived a few doors down from Jack and Eileen. I used Eileen as one of many measuring sticks to point out my physical inadequacies. As always, I felt fat, ugly, and inferior. I was totally incapable of positive internal dialogue.

To deal with my emotional pain, I ate. Classes were stressful. I ate. Marriage, sex, and finances were stressful. I ate some more. In between, I continued to mutilate my hair and skin. I also discovered bottles of hair color. Surely a new color would make me feel beautiful. Such logic!

My first semester at Oklahoma State was made memorable by my English essay class. Prior to that time, I had never written an essay or received an F. Within a week, I had accomplished both. After returning our essays, the graduate student teaching the course held me and two other rough fellows after class. She proceeded to tell us we would flunk her class, so we might as well drop then. The class was required for graduation. I was crushed. After a day of pondering the situation and crying, I indignantly marched into the office of the Chairman of the Department of English. I said I was valedictorian of my high school class and had never made an F in my life. I told him of the graduate student's remarks and that I needed help. He knowingly transferred me to the class of the benevolent Mrs. Johnson. I believe I made an F on her first essay, but she patiently had me rewrite it until I had a better grasp of the technique. Under Mrs. Johnson's kind tutelage, my grades went from C's to A's. Before the semester was over, she was reading my papers to the class as examples of creativity and form. I made an A in Mrs. Johnson's class.

As long as I stayed in my mind, I felt some small comfort. My mathematics and science professors doted on me. I loved the debate and excelled in my philosophy classes, but I ingested like manna my art history classes. After one or two courses from the art history professor, he would grade my paper, then have me grade the remainder of the students' exams. I continued to notice that my grade of a C, for one overtly seductive female art student, persisted in transforming into an A. I doubt if the professor ever read her papers. They were horrible.

In the spring of 1966, Bob graduated with a degree in political science. He went on to do two years of graduate study in the same subject. In the second year of his graduate work, I dropped out of school and worked at the college library to support us. Besides, I decided I was going to be an "Earth Mother." I had completed three years of college.

As Bob and I worked and studied, life rocked along those three years in Stillwater. We were never blissfully in love, but we were good companions. Since we both lived in our heads, our main discourse was intellectual debate. When issues arose, they and their associated feelings were not discussed. Eventually, out of total frustration, I would erupt. Bob avoided confrontation at all cost. Therefore, no difficulty was ever resolved, so I stuffed those feelings in my emotional gunnysack, along with all the others I had packed away.

In those years, the newspapers and television reports were full of the flower children, war protests, and bra burnings. On campus, there was an occasional feeble protest rally. I was relatively oblivious to the political scene and, even if I agreed with the protestors, I was too timid to join them on the picket lines.

Bob continued ROTC through college. After his graduate work, he was sent to Denver, Colorado, where he did intelligence training with the Air Force. I accompanied him and worked as a secretary in a factory where, much to my indignation, I was treated without regard for my intellect. I was just a body in a chair, shuffling papers and pounding on typewriter keys.

Bob was told he probably would not go to Vietnam, so we decided to start our family. When we happily knew I was pregnant, Bob received orders for Vietnam as did the rest of his classmates.

In the fall of 1968, before Bob left for Vietnam, we traveled in our new red Volkswagen beetle from Denver to Fort Walton Beach, Florida. In Florida, Bob trained two additional months. Along with other members of Bob's Intelligence School class, we lived in a beachfront motel. I luxuriated in my pregnancy, the beach, and no job. I enjoyed reading books, walking on the beach, body surfing in the ocean, and spending evenings with Bob, his friends, and their wives. I had never known such an active social life. While in Florida, I felt my baby's first movement. I was happy and content.

By November, Bob was in Vietnam, but being an Intelligence Officer he remained in a town distant from the fighting, so I didn't worry about his safety and had only to deal with our separation and my loneliness.

Much to my dismay, I returned to Fairfield, where I could be near our parents during my pregnancy. I rented a small two-bedroom house. There was no more country living for me. I was a city girl. The military paid for moving our belongings. By then, we had painstakingly, with minimal funds, acquired enough to furnish our home and create the most pleasant environment in which I had ever resided.

I wrote Bob daily, as he did me. For three months, I worked in the Morton library for Miss French, the librarian, for whom I had worked as a college freshman. She allowed me to continue my previous typing and filing job. In addition, she let me arrange the book displays and indulged me in art supplies. My work bore resemblance to Jackson Pollock and paint drippings. Miss French was semi-blind and delighted in my productions.

On February 12, 1969, I had a burst of energy and washed the car, cleaned the house, did laundry, and put the clothes on the line to dry. As I lay sleeping that night, my water broke and gushed all over me and the bed. I had no earthly idea what had happened. In those days, there were few books and no classes on child birth. I figured the event was a cause for concern. I stood in a dark hallway with water running down my legs and dialed my mother. There was no answer. When I called Bob's mother, Gail, she immediately picked up the phone and promptly came over and took me to the hospital. During the throes of labor, my mother arrived. She gently talked to me, wiped my face, and helped me when I had to vomit. For that brief moment in time, I felt nurtured and loved by my mother. The following afternoon, Billy arrived at 7 pounds and 4 ounces, 19 inches long, and with a head full of black hair.

Billy and I remained in the hospital five days, as all mothers and infants did in those days. On returning home, Billy and I settled into a comfortable routine. I was peaceful and content. I doted on my son. He was my joy and constant companion.

I wanted to feel pretty, so I went on another diet. I lost twenty-five pounds. I sent pictures to Bob of my new figure, and he was excited. His pet name for me was "Hunkie," which hurt my soul every time he uttered it. I made and bought new clothes. I was on top of the world. Bob was due home in November but, by the fall, my resolve broke. I began binging. I couldn't stop. I gained all the lost weight back, plus some. I was humiliated. I don't believe Bob ever forgave me.

On Bob's return, Billy was eight months old. To reunite our small family, Billy and I met him at the airport in Tulsa. From our daily letters, I felt close to Bob, but re-entry was awkward. As usual, I felt ugly. Bob's disappointment in my appearance was palpable. We never fully connected after his return. He frequently called me "Hunkie."

After Bob's Vietnam tour, the Air Force moved us to Tucson, Arizona. Before leaving, Bob, Billy, and I visited my grandparents in Arkansas. I wanted to show Grandmother Ollie her first great grandchild. From that visit, I now treasure a photograph of grandmother seated at her kitchen table with Billy on her lap. My grandfather stands behind her, and in the background is her laden oak buffet and the old pendulum clock hanging on the wall which was covered by faded floral paper. I never saw my grandmother again. Shortly thereafter, she went into the hospital for a carotid arteriogram and suffered a stroke. I didn't go to her funeral. I couldn't face the reality of her death. To this day, she remains alive in my memory, and there I visit her at will.

After we settled in Tucson, Bob continued to receive "temporary orders" for three- and four-month tours of duty in Vietnam. I was convinced he requested them and was having an affair with his Vietnamese maid. By the spring of 1970, I was twenty-three, lonely, and desperate. Any illusion I had of being an Earth

Mother had vaporized. The only way I knew to receive praise was making A's in school, so I returned to college with a vengeance. To be employable in a shrinking job market, I changed my major to chemistry and planned a Ph.D. program.

We had only one car, so I often wore jeans and old shirts, strapped Billy in the seat behind me, and bicycled him to daycare, then eight miles farther to the University of Arizona campus. When bicycling, I felt strong, capable, and self-sufficient and, to my surprise, I lost fifteen pounds. Upon discovering the weight loss, I promptly began to eat more and gain back the weight. I did this in part because of my underlying anger toward Bob for discounting me and my body.

One evening in the fall of 1971 during a biochemistry lab, I was sitting on a staircase while my experiment percolated. I listened to a 21-year-old hot-shot frat-rat boast that he was a pre-med major and applying to medical school. I casually asked him about the entrance requirements. I had them all, with A's. Right then, right there, I decided if that jerk could be a doctor, so could I. Now, that is how God works in my life. Sometimes, from the most peculiar of sources, I receive moments of blinding clarity.

I promptly consulted an academic advisor who said that with my short period of interest, it was unlikely I would be accepted the first year. Bob had been accepted to the University of Oklahoma School of Law, so I could only apply to the same school. When my acceptance letter arrived, Bob did not congratulate me. His only comment was, "Good, now I don't have to make any money." I was deeply hurt but, of course, we didn't talk about feelings.

In the spring of 1972, Bob was discharged from the Air Force. We returned to Oklahoma City and bought our first home which was located near the medical school. Bob would commute to law school in Norman. Near our home, we found a Catholic day care and school for Billy. During the following years, it was his most stable environment.

In the fall, with several other women, wives, and mothers, I entered the University of Oklahoma Medical School, and Bob entered its law school. Billy was three years old.

CHAPTER FOUR

Medical School: A Combat Zone
♀

ON THE FIRST DAY OF MEDICAL SCHOOL, they struck the fear of God into us. We were told we must pass not only our routine exams but were also required to pass Parts I, II, and III of the National Boards Licensure Examinations, which were given after our second and fourth years of medical school, and our internship year, respectively. Throughout the next five years the pressure of the Board examinations was unrelenting, as they pimped and terrorized us with their existence and each spring found us sitting for "mock" Board exams. Constantly looming over our heads was the knowledge that no matter how hard we worked, failure to pass the Boards would deny us our diplomas.

Besides my childhood, medical school was the most brutal experience of my life. The first two years consisted of class-work, labs, studying eight to twelve hours a day, and endless exams. I and 125 other students had always headed our respective classes. In a pressure cooker, we were thrown together and forced to compete with one another for the highest marks. Because I was ranked in the middle of the class, my feelings of self-worth were at an all-time low. For survival, I adopted a fellow classmate's attitude, "Good is Good Enough." I hung the slogan over my desk at home. As usual, I was depressed. As usual, with infinite wisdom, to cope with the stress, I ate. My skin erupted. I cut my hair. I ate some more. During all of my binging, I never attempted to vomit. On some level, the excess weight served a purpose.

I best learn through visual experience and, in the first year, I enjoyed and excelled in histology and anatomy classes. In histology, we learned the appearance of normal tissues of the body as viewed under the microscope and, the following year, we were taught to identify abnormal or pathological tissues.

After my acceptance into medical school, it dawned on me that I would have to take anatomy. I was gripped with fear. After some thought, I figured I could handle about anything, except dissecting the human head.

Dr. Walker, my anatomy lab professor, was a kind, learned man and a gifted teacher. For dissection, he divided us into teams, and each team was given a cadaver. Dr. Walker assigned each team member an area of the body to dissect. Of course, I was assigned the head and neck. Negotiating or requesting an exchange was foreign to my mind. Besides, I refused to appear weak in the eyes of Dr. Walker or my male classmates. I, along with other female students, insisted on proving I was the equal of any man. Whatever a man could do, I insisted on doing in spades.

Sometime during the first year, many of us bravely made our way to the morgue to view our first autopsy. There, naked on the slab, was a fair-skinned blonde-haired man in his early thirties. He looked to be in a sound sleep. On his way to work that morning, he had been killed in a car wreck. I was stunned by how instantly life could be taken. On some level, I knew there must be more to life than this brief visit.

Near the completion of anatomy class, I noticed my breasts hurt and my cups were running over. I had missed a few periods but, under stress, missing a period was normal for me. Besides, I had an IUD and had started birth control pills for my acne. It was time for my yearly pap smear, so I nonchalantly proceeded to the hospital gynecology clinic. With my legs propped in the air, I was told, by a dispassionate male resident, I was pregnant. I was numb with shock. I was a struggling, married, medical student, with a young child, an IUD, and on birth control pills. How could this be?

I told my husband the news. We talked of our thoughts but not our feelings. Two lonely islands in the same sea, we decided on an abortion. I was always the one who handled the finances. If the car needed new tires, Bob told me, and my job was to find the necessary funds. The next day, I went to the medical school's financial aid office and acquired money to pay for the procedure. After leaving the aid office, I sat on a curb, waited for a bus, and cried. My thoughts, emotions, and maternal instincts were at war. I wanted to have the baby that I believed was a girl named Laura.

Before classes the following Wednesday morning, Bob dropped me off in front of the medical school. After my classes were over, I checked myself into the hospital. I cried that night and called Bob. I wanted him to say we could work together, have the baby, and both graduate. He said nothing of the kind. I felt completely alone.

The following morning, I allowed my daughter to be taken from me by the suction pumps. Bob picked me up that evening in front of the medical school. We never spoke of the abortion. I ached and then went dead inside.

In our backyard, I planted a rose bush for Laura. I have long grieved her death.

Out of desperation, I started another diet. I had to do something to help me feel better about myself. The illusion persisted. If I was thin, I would be happy.

I passed final exams in flying colors. I survived my first year of medical school, but my marriage did not. During the abortion, when I really needed him, Bob wasn't there for me. The truth was that we had never been there for each other. We didn't know how.

In one of our final arguments, Bob said, "You are beautiful when you're mad." I was stunned. Never before had he called me beautiful. I thought, "Why did he wait until it was too late to tell me?"

That summer, Billy and I stayed with my parents. I worked in a nearby emergency room. I was the "doctor" in charge on weekends and evenings. On my first day of work, my attending physician, Dr. James, brought in a wood log covered with a sheet of synthetic material, which simulated skin. He also brought in a scalpel and suturing materials. Dr. James made a slice in the log's covering and showed me how to suture, then I was on my own. I called my log Harvey. I learned to suture on Harvey. Harvey had ants.

The emergency room was located near a large lake with heavy boating and fishing traffic. That summer, I retrieved fishhooks and sutured many a vacationer's superficial laceration. I realized that suturing skin was a lot like sewing, just different fabric. I felt the budding of confidence.

After the divorce and school starting in the fall, Bob took the car and lived in an apartment in Norman and saw Billy on weekends. Billy and I were in the house, within walking distance of his school and a bus ride from the medical school. Eventually, I was able to buy another Volkswagen.

The grueling schedule of my second year of medical school was similar to the first year, just different courses. Emotionally, I had nothing to give Billy. When I think of those times, my heart cries for my young son. He was a lonely little boy who deeply needed my love and attention, but I didn't know how to nurture him. I was never taught. To make matters worse, because of my neglect, Billy's parakeet died, and his dog ran away.

Depression was my continual state. I actually did not know I was depressed. I thought what I felt was normal. The only time I could identify depression was when I was suicidal. My classes' content was not difficult, but the amount of material to comprehend and memorize was voluminous and overwhelming. I plodded from exam to exam, interrupted only by countless hours of study. I was determined to graduate.

My most difficult course was microbiology. Memorizing the names, shapes, and reproductive patterns of bacteria defied and overloaded my memory banks. Late nights and early mornings before microbiology exams found me on my bedroom floor reviewing my numerous handwritten and color-coded study sheets.

Whatever the topic of the upcoming exam, study was accompanied with frequent binges. In an attempt to control my eating,

I kept our home devoid of my preferred binge foods—sweets. Billy was the only one who saw me binge. When the compulsion overwhelmed me, no matter what time of day or night, Billy was forced to accompany me to the donut shop, bakery, 7-11, or grocery store. A typical haul would be a dozen donuts, a sack of cookies, several candy bars, a cake, or pie, which was followed by frenzied eating and gorging myself. Bless his heart, Billy had to eat fast if he wanted any. Now, Billy doesn't care for sweets.

After reaching an all time high in my weight gain, I attended my first diet club and began weighing and measuring me and my food. Also, at a sister medical student's encouragement, I joined her in a Buddhist group that used chanting to induce a meditative state. I set up my home altar and began a daily practice. During chanting, I experienced moments of peace, clarity, and insight.

After many months, I became thin "again." I hit the relationship trail and the quest for better living through the association with testosterone. My meditation ceased. Surely, if I looked pretty and sexy, which equated in my mind with thin, I would find the right man and be loved. On the weekends, I combined men with alcohol and, under the influence, often compromised my values and risked my life. My life bore some resemblance to Diane Keaton's movie "Looking for Mr. Goodbar."

I only drank when I was thin. I was a person of extremes, either binging or rigid food control, lots of men or no men. Food, alcohol, and men provided anesthesia for my survival. Some substance or behavior was necessary for me to endure medical school and life.

FLYING SOLO

One afternoon a week in the second year, we began our clinical exposure. We each were assigned to third and fourth year medical students. Over and over, we watched them take histories and do physicals. Finally, in the latter part of the year, we were required to fly solo. I concluded that I could handle just about anything except an African-American male. As usual, God had a sense of humor and other plans.

For the examination, I wore a white coat and carried my black bag loaded with the tools of my new trade. Of course, I was assigned a 31-year-old African-American male, standing 6'5 and weighing in at about 280 pounds. I was required to examine his penis and testicles, plus a rectal exam with palpation of the prostate.

I don't know who was more scared, me or him. He was very kind and patient, without one rude remark or gesture. Methodically, I moved through each part of the examination and, to this day, I can still see him bent over the bed as I prepared to do his rectal exam. We both got through my maiden flight, and I believe we parted with each of us retaining a portion of our dignity.

PART I BOARDS

Nearing completion of my second year, Part I of National Boards and final exams were imminent. I was emotionally fried, starvation thin, and terrified of gaining weight. My binges were interspersed with food restriction or fasts but, as Boards approached, I couldn't stop binging. I couldn't sleep. I took Valium. I still couldn't sleep. I took more Valium. In those days, Valium "wasn't addictive." I was suicidal. I saw my first psychologist. He asked, "What would it take for you to commit suicide?" I answered, "Binging three days in a row."

The psychologist referred me to the Dean of Student Affairs. After discussing with the Dean the dire nature of my depression, he delayed my Board exams until later that summer. With a summer job, I studied for another two months. Without the stress of school and off Valium, my nervous system re-equilibrated. With greater mental clarity, I decided I wasn't sure what I was going to do with a medical degree, but I'd be damned if I was going to let medical school beat me. I was determined to get my degree, even if its only purpose was to decorate my bathroom wall. With that attitude, I passed the two-day examination of Part I of the National Boards.

My psychologist referred me to a psychiatrist, Dr. Snow. Over the next two years, I saw her on a regular basis. My years of silence were over. I found my voice and explored my rage toward my mother. I idealized my father. In my eyes, he could do no wrong. Dr. Snow had no children and sort of adopted me, but Dr. Snow also had an eating disorder. I felt we were trying to figure it out together, with me as the pilot study. At that time, there was no good information on the dynamics or treatment of eating disorders. Dr. Snow saved my life and was my anchor, support, and the only nurturing mother I had known.

SUMMER JOB

Throughout medical school, there was the occasional older male physician who thought women were tainting the hallowed bastion of medicine. In my second year clinicals and student rounds, Dr. Gunderson, a senior attending staff physician pontificated such an opinion. I don't believe I was intimidated. On some level, I realized Dr. Gunderson was just plain nuts. By and large, I believe I was treated fairly in my training by the opposite sex. I was my harshest critic. I demanded that I be as good as or better than any male, because I felt being a woman was a flawed condition. It was an exhausting way to live.

At that time, there were a few women on the medical school's staff, and Dr. Bathia was a wonderful example of feminine professionalism. My summer job after my second year was in the Infectious Disease Department, with Drs. Bathia and Santos. She was Hungarian, and he was of Spanish descent. They were both kind and patient.

In those days, with parental consent, children with severe handicaps could be tested with trial vaccines. To the occupants of an institution for such children, Drs. Bathia and Santos administered a test vaccine. After the vaccinations, my job was to daily monitor the children's vital signs and general health. Initially, I was repelled by those retarded, deformed children.

But needing the job and income and wanting to please Drs. Bathia and Santos, I made daily rounds on each child. There were many beds to a room. None of the children could talk, sit, crawl, walk, or hold a thermometer orally, which necessitated that all temperatures be taken rectally. The odors were abhorrent. However, over time and to my astonishment, I began to see each and every child in a new light. I felt compassion and affection for them, especially Tony.

Tony was four years old, but his body was the size of a two year old, and his head was twice the size of an adult's. Tony had hydrocephalus. He had a sweet personality and animated eyes, which he communicated with as his body rolled about the anchor of his head. One day, I came in and found Tony's eyes were glazed. The plates of his skull had collapsed inward. It was just a matter of time before he would die. I was sad. For a brief moment in time, I connected with that small child with the sparkling eyes.

THE CLINICAL YEARS

Before school started in the fall, with total lack of logic and emotional insight, I rented my home and furnishings to medical school classmates. Perhaps in search of a Bohemian lifestyle or an attempt to escape memories of Bob, I uprooted Billy and moved us into a loft apartment with my redheaded Italian boyfriend, Virgil. Virgil was a law student, and I soon discovered that he smoked marijuana heavily. Disregarding Virgil's behaviors, I set up housekeeping, filled the apartment windows with plants in hanging pots suspended by macramé, and furnished the rooms with pallets and beds. We essentially lived on the floor. Billy's bedroom looked as desolate as he did.

The third and fourth years of medical school consisted of five-week rotations on various clinical services, including, to name only a few, surgery, internal medicine, pediatrics, and psychiatry.

Psychiatry was my first rotation. My resident, Dr. Johnson, was a kind, gentle, and affirming soul. I liked talking to patients, taking histories, and trying to figure out their internal dynamics. During the first two years of medical school, Dr. Deckert, the Chairman of the Department of Psychiatry, routinely lectured on the method of taking a patient's history, and I had taken voluminous notes. By rotation on admissions, we, the medical students, were assigned patients. Our job was to take the patient's history and follow them through their hospital stay. I was assigned eighteen-year-old Jeremy, who had been admitted in his first psychotic episode and given a diagnosis of schizophrenia. Using my notes from Dr. Deckert's lectures, I repeatedly and extensively talked with Jeremy and his parents. I wanted to understand the basis of Jeremy's psychosis. At length in the hospital chart, I wrote my findings.

Dr. Johnson asked me to present my history on Jeremy at the upcoming Psychiatry Grand Rounds. I assumed that was a routine request of any third-year medical student. As always, I was nervous. I gathered even more history from Jeremy and his family. In anticipation, on the morning of the presentation, I awoke at four o'clock and further refined my notes.

As I walked into Grand Rounds, I was shocked. I didn't know what Grand Rounds were. There sat all of the medical students, interns, and residents of the psychiatry service. At the head of the table sat Dr. Deckert, all of the psychiatry professors, and Dr. Deckert's special guest, a professor visiting from Harvard.

When Dr. Deckert asked Dr. Johnson for his case presentation, Dr. Johnson turned the podium over to me. Dr. Deckert was irate and began to criticize Dr. Johnson for having a third-year medical student present in Grand Rounds. Dr. Johnson affirmed his decision saying, "Please allow her to present."

Dr. Deckert was somewhat mollified and motioned for me to proceed. I began to read my lengthy hand-written notes. The room was silent. When I finished, Dr. Deckert asked me how I learned to take such a history. Abashed at his question, I answered the simple truth, "From you." Dr. Deckert was obviously pleased. He began to extol my presentation to all in attendance.

He reprimanded his residents and stated he expected a similar performance from them in their next Grand Rounds presentation. Thereafter, Dr. Deckert and I had a special bond.

Unfortunately, my experiences on the remaining rotations were not as pleasant. On these rotations, we were organized into teams that included a resident, intern, and several third- and fourth-year medical students. We wore white coats and stethoscopes and made daily rounds on all of the team's patients. These rounds were punctuated by we medical students being bullied, battered, and humiliated for our fledgling store of medical knowledge. The more I was battered, the more fearful I became, and the less I could remember. Of course, there was always someone busting their gonads to recite the answers like a wind-up robot for the "Jock Doc" award.

As medical students, we performed the history and physical exams on newly hospitalized patients. We were free labor and the low people on the totem pole. I always knew I was getting the vilest job on the ward when the resident or intern predicated it as "a learning experience."

During Thanksgiving in my third year, I was on my surgery rotation when I learned Bob was to marry. I was devastated. I still loved him and harbored hope that we would again be together. I was a size six. I turned to my old enemy, disguised as a friend, food.

I was desperate for relief. I ingested huge quantities, and often, while no one was looking, the food came from half-eaten patient trays. Those unscreened trays could have been from anyone, including patients with tuberculosis. I had to have emotional relief at any cost. Thank goodness AIDS had yet to present itself.

On the surgery service, I awoke at four in the morning and often did not return home until ten at night. Every third night I was on call and spent the night in the hospital. Sleep was a rare commodity. Because of my work hours, my son went to live with his father and his new wife, Molly. Billy never wanted to live with me again. He blamed and resented me for the divorce. I felt shame for my inadequacies as a mother.

During five of the ten weeks on the surgery service, I had a particularly vicious chief resident, Dr. Gravitz. Dr. Gravitz took delight in carving up medical students. One Sunday afternoon, Virgil was smoking pot. I decided to try it and, with great bravado, I deeply inhaled a few puffs and proceeded to a shopping mall. Soon after entering the mall, I became disoriented, confused, and had an unsteady gait. Carefully, I made my way home.

The following day, I scrubbed in with Dr. Gravitz on a cholecystectomy, removal of a gallbladder. Normally, I would study extensively about the procedure. Unaware that I was still under the influence of the marijuana and without cracking a book, I boldly strolled into the surgery suite. I held retractors to expose the operating site, while Dr. Gravitz and the intern operated. Upon discovering that I was unprepared, Dr. Gravitz drilled me unmercifully about every aspect of the surgical procedure and, when I answered incorrectly, he ridiculed me and hammered me with more questions. I cried but kept pulling on those damn retractors. I never again smoked marijuana or went into surgery unprepared. A few years later, I learned Dr. Gravitz died from alcoholism and drug addiction. I guess he lived in his own private hell.

My binging was like wildfire. Unable to stop, I had to deal with the surgery service and my expanding, miserable body. I gained fifty pounds in five weeks. No one asked if I needed help. Staff and fellow medical students just looked on in disbelief.

From the shame and embarrassment of my weight gain, I asked Virgil to move out. I told him of my revulsion for my body and that I couldn't bear for him to see or touch me. Virgil was surprised. He had been so stoned, he hadn't noticed my weight gain.

Following surgery rotation and humiliation over my weight, I took a five-week leave of absence and considered dropping out of school. I spent hours alone in a dark apartment in a semi-catatonic state, leaving the apartment only to obtain food. I felt too ugly to exist and thought daily of suicide. My two attempts as a teenager were spur-of-the-moment decisions. By now, I had contemplated suicide for years. I planned a gunshot wound to the head or abdomen and knew I would be successful, so I had to be sure I wanted to die. I held on to life by a thread.

Danna was my only friend. She was a happy obese law student and visited me in my seclusion. I watched her laugh, smile, and function. I finally decided if Danna could exist in the world fat, so could I. Previously, I had refused to purchase clothes "until I lost weight." I made myself go shopping and buy an attractive wardrobe that fit. Thank heavens for Penney's. It suited my budget. In flattering attire, I returned to school.

I proceeded through my rotations. The hours were long, with frequent call nights and tired, grumpy residents, but no service equaled the torture of surgery.

On my pediatrics rotation, I found it difficult to watch children of all ages in pain, especially the children with cancer. I watched the shocked and bewildered faces of parents whose children had just been diagnosed with leukemia. Because their child had not felt well, they had just come in for a simple blood test, only to be told the horrifying news. I hurt seeing the children without hair, with distended abdomens and wasted limbs. On night call, I was often called to restart IVs on one of these small, fragile bodies. Sometimes, I wanted to say to the parents, "It is time to let go. Your child is being tortured by these needles and poisons." But I kept silent. It was not my place to speak such words. The oncologists should have, but they grimly pursued their chemicals and protocols. They seemed to have hardened themselves against the children's pain. I could not.

MY NICHE

During these two years of clinical rotations, I saw Billy on weekends and, occasionally, he spent the night with me. On these visits, I picked him up and returned him to Bob and Molly's house. Molly was kind, loving, nurturing, and everything I thought a wife and mother should be. I cried every time I saw that little family of three, which did not include me. I questioned, "Why couldn't I be like Molly?" When I was with Billy, I was emotionally unavailable and felt inadequate. Actually, I wasn't emotionally available for anyone, including myself. I was a walking robot locked in survival mode.

In the spring of my senior year, I did an elective rotation in Pathology at Baptist Medical Center in Oklahoma City. By then, my spirit and body were bloodied and beaten beyond recognition. During that rotation, I didn't have to deal with patients, write orders, or be badgered by demanding residents. I sat in a small, quiet, windowless office, read pathology textbooks, and looked through the microscope at slides mounted with thin slices of brightly stained tissues. The tissues had been surgically removed from patients in the operating rooms across the hall from the pathology department. In the pathologists' offices, I sat and listened as the surgeons and pathologists discussed a patient's case. The surgeons politely asked the pathologist about the diagnosis of the tissue they had removed, because the diagnosis determined what further surgical procedures and treatment were indicated. The surgeons hands were tied without the pathologist's report. There was divine justice.

Occasionally, I accompanied one of the two pathology residents down to the morgue in the hospital basement and observed him perform an autopsy. My senses were assaulted as I watched a human body being cut from stem to stern and all its organs sliced and diced. As always, I numbed my feelings and went straight to my head. As I asked questions, the pathology residents answered courteously and explained procedures. Little did I know that they wanted junior residents to take over the autopsy service.

The Chairman of the Department, Dr. Hensley, was a good, kind man and welcomed me to apply for one of the department's residency positions. I had found my niche.

After completing my pathology rotation, I returned to the University of Oklahoma Medical School Campus to complete my remaining rotations. I went back to the diet club and shrank to a size six. I was anorexic and terrorized by the thought of gaining weight. In addition, no matter how well I did on my rotations, I lived in horror of the possibility that I might make "A MISTAKE" and fail to graduate. Prior to graduation, I also had a foreboding that I would die of leukemia or a brain tumor. I had been told since infancy, in words and deeds, that I was less than nothing and did not deserve to exist. For me to succeed was out of the question. As I neared the demolition of those childhood tapes, I was stressed to the breaking point.

It was the spring of 1976. Part II of the National Boards was scheduled before graduation. I began to binge and couldn't stop. Again, I was severely depressed and suicidal, so Dr. Snow hospitalized me. Delivered by a friend, I entered the hospital with stacks of exam study books in tow. My obsession to eat was overwhelming. I hit the hospital snack bar candy machines, sneaked food to my room in the pockets of my robe, and continued to binge. The nurses found the wrappers hidden in the bottom of my wastebasket. I was busted.

Dr. Snow restricted my food—shades of my mother. In desperation, I walked off the ward and out of the hospital. At the nearest convenience store, I loaded up on candy bars and headed home on foot, some twelve miles away. Halfway there, crying, I called Bob and told him what happened. He had received similar calls from me before. He picked me up and took me home.

One day at a time, I made it through that spring. I stopped binging and restricted my food even more. With Dr. Snow's help, my Boards were delayed. I studied another two months and passed them in the summer after graduation.

When the day came to don my cap and gown, my parents, accompanied by a rainstorm, rushed into town, late, in chaos, and ill-humored. In spite of them, I proudly walked across the stage and claimed my coveted degree. I had finally broken the tapes. I was a success. I had graduated from medical school, but I did not live happily ever after.

CHAPTER FIVE

Pathology Residency

♀

AFTER GRADUATION, I WAS A NEW M.D.—fresh off the assembly line. I was thin and starting over, or so I thought. I sold my house and everything I owned, moved into an apartment, and bought a sports car, a British Leydig TR7, my graduation present to myself. Surely with a small car, I wouldn't allow myself to gain weight. I might not fit into it. My food restricting became worse. I was starving.

That July at Baptist Medical Center in Oklahoma City, I began my internship which consisted of six months of clinical rotations, followed by six months of pathology service. During my clinicals, my attending physicians were fairly congenial and patient, except for one very egotistical cardiologist, but even he wasn't that difficult. I spent two months on the hematology and oncology service. Up close and personal, I saw patients with cancer, their treatment, and their death. Compared to medical school, my internship rotations were minimally stressful, but my ability to cope with any stress was nonexistent. In fact, just being alive was stressful for me. Once more I began to binge and was more out of control than ever. To prevent my eating,

I took no money or checks to work, and credit cards weren't a big item in those days. By ten in the morning, I had to leave work, go home and get my checkbook, hit the convenience food stores, and return to work. I was a drug addict, and my drug was food.

Filled with shame, I rarely binged in public but ate in my car. At work, I binged in the only private place, the bathroom stalls. On hospital call-nights, I went to the basement snack bar, spent all of my money, engulfed my purchases, and then made my way up the twelve floors of the hospital and the corresponding patient food areas. I lived alone in dark places. I gained sixty-five pounds in six months and was down to one tight-fitting blue dress. I attempted to hide my bulging body under a white coat and, with great effort, I contorted my body to sit in the TR7. It fit like a corset.

Dr. Snow had semi-retired and moved to a rural town ninety miles away. On occasion, I drove the distance for a therapy session, but I had long realized that neither she nor I could fix me.

I felt embarrassed and humiliated by the devastation I had once again wrought on my body and couldn't bear to face Dr. Hensley or the other members of the pathology department. They liked me, and I couldn't tolerate the all-too-familiar look of shock on their faces. I had ballooned, seemingly overnight, from a size six to a sixteen. On the night before my first day of the six-month pathology rotation, which was to be followed by another three years of pathology residency, I again took an overdose of pills. I awoke with a horrible hangover, put on my blue dress covered by my white coat, and went to work. Throughout my life, I put on the best face I could muster, which often didn't look like much, and went to work. Work saved my life. It kept me going when I felt I had no other reason to live.

I have a photograph taken of me in that blue dress. My face and downcast eyes are the picture of depression. For over four years I had been in the medical community, among physicians, residents, and nurses, and never once had anyone said, "You look depressed. I think you need help." The lack of recognition of my condition says a lot about the powers of observation and the mental health of the medical profession.

The following three-and-a-half years in pathology training consisted of my occupying a windowless, closed-door cubicle, reading textbooks and journals, and looking through the microscope at stained tissue on slides. These tasks were interrupted only by going to one of several labs, the morgue, lectures, or Tumor Board.

MORE BOARDS

In the spring of 1977, nearing the completion of my internship year, I was to sit, along with the other interns in the state, for Part III of the National Boards. Passing this third examination was necessary before we received our Oklahoma Medical License and State and Federal Drug Licenses. I was so emotionally compromised that the idea of sitting for another Board examination was intolerable. Again, I delayed the exam, studied for another two months, traveled to Dallas—the closest test site—and sat for the two-day examination. I wore my blue dress, covered by a white coat. To endure the stress, I binged before, during, and after each test segment, but I passed.

Throughout pathology residency, board examinations again loomed over my head. In pathology, one can train four years in anatomical, four years in clinical, or two years in each. To be more marketable, I choose to do the latter, which meant I had to sit for two Board exams.

ANATOMICAL TRAINING

The first two years of training were in anatomical pathology. Another resident, Walt, and I examined and dissected most of the surgical specimens received in the tissue lab. On arrival in the lab, the tissue specimens were placed in formalin preservative, logged in, and assigned a number. The specimens ranged from fragments of tissue, in the case of biopsies, to whole body parts. Walt or I carefully examined and described into a dictaphone the measurements, weights, and appearance of each specimen, and selected appropriate tissue samples for slide preparation.

I dissected hundreds of total mastectomies and selected tissue samples from the primary cancer site, then serially sectioned and sampled the remaining breast tissue for additional abnormalities. The mastectomy specimen included the auxiliary contents, from which lymph nodes were harvested. As I dissected that fallen part of a woman, I felt empathy for its owner.

I examined countless portions of stomachs and colons, with abnormalities ranging from ulcers or diverticuli to ugly ulcerating cancers. I dissected innumerable whole kidneys and lobes of lungs containing cancers. I examined an endless number of ovaries and uteri, which contained anything from benign fibroids to cancers of the endometrium, cervix, or ovaries. Each specimen was accompanied by some history on the patient, even if it was only the age and gender. From the cancer type, location, size, and extent of invasion, I knew something about the length of life probable for the person whose organ I was examining, and I felt their mortality.

I examined traumatically amputated limbs, limbs removed from diabetics, portions of bones or limbs removed for cancers, fragments of skin and hair from facelifts, and testicles and penises removed for sex changes. The march of human parts through the tissue lab was endless and, on a primarily subconscious level, I was deeply impacted by those marching body parts.

Samples of tissues were placed in small plastic cassettes. In the cassettes, the tissue was processed and impregnated with paraffin. The paraffin blocks were then chilled and, with a razor sharp blade, sliced into transparent shavings, which were placed on a glass slide. The tissue-mounted slides were stained and covered by a thin layer of glass and were then ready for examination under the microscope.

The pathologist's job is to identify cellular abnormalities of tissue and categorize these cellular abnormalities by a diagnosis. In the first year of my residency, I reviewed all the slides processed by the lab and the pathologist's corresponding reports. In my closed cubicle, I spent endless hours peering through the microscope. As I viewed life on a cellular level, I dissociated from my reality and lived in a world of thought, color, and pattern.

As Walt and I advanced in our training, we reviewed the slides before the pathologist and dictated the reports and diagnoses. Afterwards, the pathologist reviewed our findings, made the necessary corrections, and signed off on the case.

In these first two years of our residency, Walt or I performed all of the autopsies that were requested in the hospital. When it was my turn and the autopsy request came, I descended to the bowels of the hospital and, with an assistant, dissected a human body. I did autopsies on almost every imaginable medical condition. Seemingly devoid of emotion, surrounded by the stench of death, and elbow-deep in blood and dead body parts, I weighed, sectioned, and examined each organ and retained appropriate specimens for histologic examination. Later, with the surfacing of my childhood memories, I realized how psychically traumatized I was by these autopsies.

SURGICAL HELP

In the second year of training, I moved to a cheaper furnished apartment, which looked as dismal as I felt. My weight climbed to an all-time high of 216 pounds, and my depression became worse than ever. I went to work, abused my body with food, and attempted to sleep the remaining hours of my life. I was disappointed each time I awoke. I had lost faith in therapy, diets, and diet clubs, and I knew without help I would be dead by my own hands within six months. I knew of only one remaining option—surgery.

In the fall of 1977, I took a one-week "vacation" and had an intestinal bypass in a neighboring hospital. Besides the surgeons and attending hospital staff, only one friend knew of my surgery. I returned to work the following Monday with a newly stitched vertical surgical incision extending the length of my abdomen.

I went about my work as if nothing had happened, which was typical of me. With a fourteen-inch incision and without medication, I disclosed to no one that I was in pain. I was very practiced in this behavior. Actually, I felt the first hope I had known for years. I would have borne any physical pain if it extricated me from my emotional hell.

I knew I was improving when I did not sleep every hour of the day that I was not working or eating. I felt I had made tremendous strides when I was able to turn on the television and watch a program or do needlepoint. A few months later, I moved into a more cheerful apartment and bought furniture, a sign I was contemplating a future.

My surgery bypassed a large portion of my small intestine and made it unavailable for the absorption of nutrients. The remaining portion of small bowel available for food absorption was unable to handle the volume of food it received and passed it on to the large intestine for excretion. The bypass allowed me unrestricted eating without fear of weight gain, and I even began to lose weight. Over the next year, even though I continued to binge, I shrank to a relatively normal size. However, a considerable portion of each day was occupied by contemplation on the bathroom throne secondary to the fifteen to twenty bowel movements required to eliminate the undigested food coursing through my alimentary tract.

My spirits were lifting, and I developed a few women friends and participated in some of their activities. On New Year's Eve of 1977, we gathered at one of their homes for a sleep-over, and the hostess had laid in an ample supply of champagne. Being unfamiliar with the effects of champagne and without a single thought that I was on autopsy call, I imbibed a goodly amount of that liquid. The following morning, I awoke with a horrific hangover and was chagrined to discover I had four bodies lined up for autopsy in the hospital morgue. In a foul mood, I slogged through the most autopsies I ever performed in a single day. One has to chortle at the humor of my dilemma.

Longing for male attention, I attended a church singles group and met Dan, who also led an isolated, detached life. I had again found another island in my ocean. Our courting was relatively devoid of romance and included Sunday dinners with Dan's schizophrenic mother. But coming from such isolation, I found even Sunday afternoons entertaining. Desperate for love and companionship, I asked Dan to marry me. He said, "Yes."

We married in the fall of 1978 in the Baptist Hospital Chapel. The wedding was a solitary affair, with only his mother and a mutual friend attending. I thereupon moved into Dan's new home, which had four bedrooms, four bathrooms, and the two of us. Anyone with insight—of which I had none—would have known something was amiss when, on our wedding night, I required champagne before bedding. Wine and champagne became my frequent sexual lubricant with Dan.

My third and fourth years of pathology residency were in the clinical laboratory where we learned the theory, technique, instrumentation, and interpretation of all the tests performed on body fluids, including blood, urine, and cerebral spinal fluids. We were also taught how to perform and interpret bone marrow biopsies. The clinical portion also included the microbiology laboratory, my area of least interest.

During the third year, I led some semblance of a normal life, but continued to binge. As always, I binged in secret. The bathroom off the kitchen was my private eating closet. Unknown to Dan, I kept my stash in the bathroom's cabinet, beneath the sink.

I decided I needed to lose more weight, and Dan took no issue with my decision. He felt I had found an ingenious method of weight control. With another week's "vacation," I had another surgery, revising the intestinal bypass and shortening the section of functioning small bowel that absorbed food. Again on Monday, I returned to work as if nothing had happened. Years later, I understood why I could put on a mask of normalcy in the face of significant life events.

I was called twice over the next year to do an autopsy on a patient who had died from complications of an intestinal bypass. On each occasion, I traded with Walt for another case. I could not face the morgue slab and the dead body that could have been mine.

After my body had been a normal size for over a year, I began to experience an unfamiliar feeling, a desire to live. I was even making plans for the future and wanted a baby.

I became pregnant. At thirty-three, the hormonal shifts and my body's surgically compromised state made this pregnancy much more difficult than my previous two. I stayed in a perpetual state of green. Once, on stating how sick I was, Walt retorted, "What's the big deal, it's just hormones." I nearly decked him.

Sadly, I lost the baby in the fourth month and knew it was because of the bypass. Besides the loss of the baby, I was experiencing symptoms of declining health secondary to malnutrition.

Later, while on an all-protein diet, my electrolytes became so unbalanced, while preparing for bed one night, I passed out nude in my walk-in closet and defecated on myself. When Dan later found me in a semiconscious state, he washed and dressed me, then rushed me to the hospital emergency room for intravenous fluid replacement.

As I continued to sit on the stool during my series of daily bowel movements, I knew I had to have the bypass reversed if I wanted to live a normal life span, but I was terrified of another massive weight gain.

I talked with my surgeon and agreed to reverse my intestinal bypass and reconstitute my small bowel to its full absorptive capacity, if he agreed during the procedure to perform a stomach stapling. The latter procedure created a small gastric pouch which supposedly limited the amount of food I could ingest at any one time. In the winter of 1979, I took another week's "vacation," and the fourteen-inch incision was again made in the same site of the two previous surgeries. I returned to work the following Monday—an X-ray of my abdomen now lights up like a Christmas tree with metal footprints of my body's abuse.

While healing from the last procedure, I overfilled my stomach pouch and, by January 1980, I could again consume huge quantities of food at a single sitting and had no protective barrier between my body size and my compulsion to overeat. I was powerless over food and gripped with fear. During an airplane flight a month before my last surgery, I read of a spiritual program that might help someone like me. With no other alternative, I tried God. In desperation, I dove headlong into my spiritual journey, which continues to this day.

After all of the therapy, surgeries, diets, and diet clubs I could stomach, literally and figuratively, looking to God or a Higher Source to help me with my compulsion to eat was definitely a new concept. As far as food and my weight were concerned and eventually many other aspects of my life, I had to admit complete defeat.

All I knew was that I needed help. After trying everything else, I might as well try God. On some level, I knew if I wanted to connect with God, I needed to pray. One day, at home alone, I locked the door of my bathroom, so no one would see me. Impeccable reasoning! As I kneeled, I felt like my knees were rusty hinges. In my first prayer in over a decade, I said, "God, you son of a bitch, if you are up there, I need some help." Even with that degree of belief, help came.

APPROVAL

During my last two years of residency, Dr. Hensley groomed me to manage a rural hospital-based laboratory in the western Oklahoma town of Clanton. I was to add a tissue lab to the existing laboratory which analyzed blood, urines, and other body fluids. The hospital administration and staff, Dr. Hensley, and I hoped to create a regional cancer referral center. At the height of the oil boom, in the spring of 1980, I signed a yearly six-figure contract to be the pathologist in Clanton.

Surely, now I had arrived, and my father would approve of me. My parents came to visit, but my father did not acknowledge my accomplishment and made me wait on him like a five-and-dime waitress. I was devastated.

With my parents asleep in one of the four bedrooms, I drove to the grocery store and bought a pie, a cake, and a sack of cookies. I planned to eat it all. Barely scratching the surface, I started crying. I awoke Dan and told him what I had done. With concern, he stood beside me as I cried and fed the junk to the appropriate receptacle, the garbage disposal. I realized that night, no matter what my successes, my father would never approve of me, and I might as well stop trying to please him.

I believed the only way I could stop binging was to abstain from all foods containing a significant amount of sugar. I also knew I had to abstain from alcohol because if I drank, I couldn't stop eating. As my body began to withdraw from the large quantities of sugar it was accustomed to processing, my every waking thought was consumed with craving for sweets. For months, on my route to and from work each day, to avoid stopping at a store for my binge foods, I prayed and focused on the white stripes in the middle of the road.

One Sunday after six weeks without sugar, Dan was driving us home from church, and my compulsion to binge became so intense, I prayed and held on to the edge of the seat as if my life depended on it, because it did. I thought, "Normal people don't have these thoughts. The way I think must be a form of insanity."

After six months without sugar, I realized for the first time in my life the obsession to binge had lifted and the only thing I had done differently from all the previous "diets" was pray. In that moment of clarity, I was convinced there had to be something pretty powerful about this God deal.

I was afraid to trust a God I didn't understand. What if God wanted to change my life in a manner that was unacceptable to me? However, the way my life was going, I didn't have a lot to lose. Slowly, I began to turn my life piecemeal over to God. I would give God a problem that I couldn't solve and then marvel at God's ingenious solution. As God's success far exceeded my own, I became willing to turn more and more of my life over to God's care. Plus, I had a deal with God. If I turned my life over to God's care, it was God's job to take care of me. Through this process, I realized that I can't understand an Infinite God with my finite mind.

During this period, I also realized that I always worked hard for second best, but my God wants the best for me. However, to receive what God has in store for me, I have to let go of control and give all of me to God. I once asked, "Is there anything (of the old me) I can keep." I was told, "If there is anything you can keep, we'll let you know." There wasn't. I had to let go of everything, but what God had in store for me far exceeded my wildest imagination.

EVEN MORE BOARDS

In January of 1980, I took a Board review course in Kansas City. Even though I knew I wasn't quite ready, I flew to Atlanta in March of that year and sat for the three-day examination in Anatomical and Clinical Pathology. I failed both exams and was embarrassed and disappointed, but God picked me up by my spiritual collar, shook me off, and I went at it again. I knew the anatomical segment would be my easiest, so I studied several months, traveled to the examination site in South Carolina, and passed with flying colors. The clinical portion could wait until we moved to Clanton.

In August of 1980, at the age of thirty-four, I completed my pathology residency. I was finally a grown-up and could practice independently in my chosen profession. With a new career ahead of me and Dan mobilizing his exploration geology business, we moved to our new rural home.

CHAPTER SIX

My First Career

♀

WITH EXCITEMENT AND ANTICIPATION for our future and our simple pastoral life, Dan and I moved to Clanton. As a highly skilled physician, I anticipated that I would be respected and accepted into the community, but I soon remembered the lessons of Fairfield.

Prior to our move to Clanton, the hospital hired a technologist and bought the necessary equipment to set up the tissue lab. Immediately upon my arrival, the lab was operational, and I began my duties as a pathologist.

Working in a hospital-based office, I took an active role with the hospital staff. I soon realized the monthly fourteen-member physician staff meetings were the site of warring egos. Two Middle-Eastern brothers led the pack of the least informed with the loudest mouths. The native Clantonite gynecologist was vicious to all, especially to me and his newly arrived Asian competitor. Another Clantonite patriarch, in his rapidly approaching senility, held court and endlessly pontificated. The Doctors of Medicine looked down on the two Doctors of Osteopathy. The two Guatemalan surgeons were well trained but added their

Latino volatility. The Mennonite orthopedist looked on with disdain. Being the only female physician, I was doomed in my attempt to add organization, reason, and manners to the three-ringed circus called "staff meetings."

As an educated woman from the city, I was regarded with much suspicion by the locals. Clanton had a rich oil and wheat-farming elite who were well traveled and often well educated but, to be included in their sphere, one had to marry or be born into it. Once again, I was an outsider, as were many of the foreign-born physicians and their wives, so we befriended each other.

After my rearing, I swore I would never again live on a farm, but something deep in me yearned to return to the land. After becoming established in the community, I hoped for Dan and me to be able to buy and live on several acres, but my plans got side-tracked by money and my desire for prestige.

Prior to our move, Dan and I commissioned the construction of a modest custom-built home located near the hospital. After being in Clanton a few months, I was making a monthly five figure income. On some level, I decided that if my home was lavish enough, perhaps I would be accepted by the local upper crust. So I began to buy expensive furniture and "decorate."

In the meantime, to help me with my eating disorder, I continued to practice daily prayer and meditation, and I located spiritual support groups in Clanton and surrounding towns. I maintained an anorexic size six by days and weeks of restrictive meals in which I measured everything I ate and counted every almighty calorie. These meals were interrupted by an occasional two-hour binge. Since I abstained from eating sugar, I switched food obsessions, and a typical binge was a large bag of chips or eight to twelve ounces of cashews. After suitable emotional self-flagellation for my indiscretions, I would hoist myself back on the wagon for another round.

On the Friday night of February 6th, 1981, out of deep emotional pain, I cried out, "God help me." On the outside, by society's standards, I was a success but, on the inside, I had such a hole in my gut I didn't even give God a suggestion how to fill it.

Twenty-four hours later, our phone rang. At a staff meeting a few months earlier, I mentioned that Dan and I might want to adopt. Dr. Haynes had just delivered a baby girl who was available for adoption. He asked, "Do you want her?" I said, "Yes, but I better ask my husband. I will call you right back." Within thirty minutes, Dan and I were at the hospital viewing our new daughter, Sarah Anne. Of Navajo descent, Sarah had beautiful brown skin and a head full of straight black hair. The next morning found Dan and me wheeling our cart through Target and filling it with every item we could think of to care for our daughter. We brought Sarah home that afternoon. The hole in my gut never returned.

I doted on Sarah but had few nurturing skills. From the information of my rearing, I thought a young child had little mental awareness, akin to a vegetable, and just required basic physical care. Thank goodness for Sarah, I found Mrs. Crawford, a kindly grandmotherly soul, to care for her while I worked. Between "Crawford," as Sarah later called her, and Dan, Sarah blossomed.

With a new baby and a full-time work schedule, I studied for my clinical pathology Boards. Spring found me on the Florida coast, occupying a seedy hotel room where the exam was to be held. In depressed isolation before, during, and after the examination, I performed my ritual of binging on nuts and chips. Again, I did not pass, and I knew it was because of my weakness in microbiology.

After the exam, life meandered its slow course. Without a deep emotional bond, Dan and I were primarily companions. With Sarah's arrival, she became Dan's world. They became a twosome, with me peering in. I wanted Dan to show me the affection he bestowed on Sarah, but I was not graced in kind.

Billy was twelve years older than Sarah, and he enjoyed her about as much as any older brother going through puberty usually enjoys a younger sibling. Billy resisted visiting us in Clanton but, in an effort to develop some relationship with my son, I insisted he do so one weekend a month. Sarah, Dan, and I looked forward to Billy's visit, but Billy resented being taken from his friends and weekend activities.

Throughout this period, I continued to pray and ask for spiritual help and guidance to relieve me of the tyranny of my obsession with food. One day while binging, I looked down into Sarah's face, as she crawled on the floor, and knew I had to stop. I didn't want my daughter to be subjected to my insanity with food. To stop binging, I released my mealtime rigidity, ceased counting calories, and adopted some semblance of normal eating patterns. Slowly, my size far exceeded a six but was maintained within a healthy range and, to tolerate my body size and prevent binging out of self-hate, I refrained from weighing and measuring myself and wore only loose clothes.

Self-hate had been my constant companion for many years. Then I heard someone say, "Selfishness is not thinking well of oneself but thinking constantly of oneself." I knew they had read my mail, because I carried on a continual internal self-depreciating dialogue over my perceived mental and physical shortcomings. I especially used the ever ready scales and measuring tape as witnesses to my failures. I later decided that scales were best buried or run over by a truck and cutting or burning tape measures worked nicely.

During my time in Clanton, I began my long arduous task of re-messaging myself and reclaiming my power from a number as the determinate of my worth. I acted as if I loved and respected myself regardless of my age, size, shape, or weight. I was told affirmations worked and, even if I didn't believe them, to "Say them anyway." Daily, for several years I looked in the mirror and into my eyes and said, "I love you...You are beautiful...God loves you." I worked to identify my self-negating thoughts and actions and to choose positive thoughts and behaviors in their stead. Now, I know the subconscious mind hears and manifests everything we tell ourselves, so we must be very careful how we talk to everyone, especially ourselves.

Though working to evolve emotionally and spiritually, I took a detour through conspicuous consumption. The historical home of a widowed elite Clantonite came on the market. I snatched it up as my dream home and proceeded to decorate its three floors even more profusely than I had our previous home. I filled every room with beautiful pieces of furniture. The floors were covered with oriental rugs so expensive I avoided walking on them. I filled cabinet upon cabinet with china, crystal, and works of art. Surely now, I would be included as a member of the Clanton aristocracy. Wrong. As usual, I was snubbed. I was still that frightened little girl begging for daddy's approval.

The County Medical Examiner

Being the only pathologist in eighty miles, I became the county medical examiner. In this role, two calls stand sentinel in my mind. The first was to view a body found in a field. During my drive to the site, I prayed for courage. The bloated, maggot-ridden African-American body in female attire was displayed for my review. The sheriff and his deputies were waiting for me to heave, but with great bravado while inwardly gagging, I completed my investigation and managed to banter with the men. The body was taken to Oklahoma City for autopsy by the state medical examiner. We were later told the body was that of a man, who had been strangled. I suppose one of the bubbas refused to allow the poor tortured soul space on the planet.

On another occasion, I was called to a local motel room. The room was scattered with empty liquor bottles and, on the bed, lay a man in peaceful repose bearing a discrete bullet hole to the temple. His image haunted me. I had long contemplated barricading myself in a similar room, eating myself into oblivion, and exiting in the same fashion. I longed for the peace I saw on his face.

Free At Last

I was binge free for over a year and, in the spring of 1982, I began a very thorough daily regimented study for my clinical Boards. I pocketed my pride and contacted a Ph.D. in microbiology who taught in a neighboring community college and made him a lucrative offer for private tutoring. For the next several months, we met on a weekly basis. I knew I was ready and, in the fall, I flew to San Diego. The day before the exam, I continued to review my notes. I was honed like an Olympic athlete. After dinner that evening, I crossed the hotel lobby and heard music lilting from the bar and was overcome by an intense compulsion to get drunk. It never entered my mind that if I got drunk I would blow the exam, but I knew if I drank I couldn't stop eating. I began to pray, and not a drop of alcohol passed my lips. The next morning I was clear-minded, rested, and ready to go. After completion of the second day's examinations, I had a bounce in my step because I knew I had passed. For the first time in ten years, I didn't have a Board exam hovering over me like a dark cloud.

Without the looming threat of Boards, our lives followed a peaceful course. Sarah prospered. My work was somewhat fulfilling. Dan and I were congenial with each other but, without emotional intimacy, the bed we shared had an unspoken line down the middle, which neither of us breached. Each night when he came to bed, I pretended to be asleep. I didn't want him to touch me.

Even with our lack of intimacy, Dan and I hoped to adopt again. We refused several Caucasian babies in hopes of receiving a child of similar coloring to Sarah. With Dan's and my pale hair and skin, we didn't want Sarah to be the only family member with nature's tan. In the spring of 1983, we were told we might be allowed to adopt a Hispanic mother's infant, who was due to arrive in a month. I prayed for God's will to prevail and, on May 22nd, the call came. In haste, we found our way to another rural hospital to view our son, Jeffrey, with brown hair and eyes with the longest eyelashes I had ever seen. Dan and I were content with our two beautiful children, who were the center of our world together.

CHANGE

The oil boom ended with a thud and with it the dream of a regional cancer treatment center. Also, new federal legislation had affected the practice of pathology so severely it was impossible for me to continue a small solo practice. I went job hunting.

I felt a year in an academic setting might improve my marketability, so I peppered the teaching hospitals with resumes and interviewed in Dallas and New York City. The latter was more of an adventure for me than a serious consideration of such a drastic relocation of our family.

My New York interview was my first trip to that city, so I wanted to do it up right. I stayed in a lovely hotel on Fifth Avenue and shopped in Bloomingdale's and Saks. I enjoyed the city's smorgasbord of sights, sounds, and smells. I had an uneventful interview at Mount Sinai Hospital, but my visit was made memorable by the Metropolitan Museum of Art and its Impressionist collection, especially the superb sculptures by Degas. In addition, the museum had on exhibit a twenty-five-year collection of a male Parisian designer. I was enlightened. Most of the clothes were created for flat-chested, prepubertal, anorexic females or males. The collection did not contain a single garment to fit the form of a healthy adult woman. Was this what I aspired to look like with all of my dieting?

My job search continued. Since my move to Clanton, Dr. Hensley had retired from Baptist Medical Center. After lolling a short time, he was asked to be the Interim Chairman for the Department of Pathology at the University of Oklahoma School of Medicine, a position he was to occupy for the next three years.

Over some faculty dissent because of my lack of "academic train-ing," Dr. Hensley hired me for a one-year instructorship position.

In the summer of 1984, Dan and I left our large Clanton home, scaled down our living expenses, and moved our family to Oklahoma City. After settling into a rented home, I reconnected with my spiritual groups.

For three years, I had been a normal size, and my eating disor-der had been in remission, which meant that I was without sugar consumption or binges. Through prayer, meditation, and my spiritual support groups, I began to deal with life on its terms. My spiritual process was one of recognizing that I was powerless over food, people, places, and things and turning my life over to God's care. I learned to pray for the knowledge of God's will for me and the strength to follow that will, which eliminated a laun-dry list of my wants. I discovered God supplied all of my needs, which did not always coincide with my wants. I also worked on releasing old ideas that no longer served my higher good. I used prayer in all times, places, and situations and then became quiet and waited for God's answer to be revealed. The answer might come from the words of another, a situation that just "happened" to evolve, or through my intuition or inner voice. I knew it was no mistake that my mentor, Dr. Hensley, was again my supervi-sor. He always gave me validation and wise counsel.

To prove my academic wings, I hit the ground running. My research partner was Dr. Lawrence DeBault, who had the repu-tation of having the personality of a "viper," but Larry and I hit it off beautifully. Among his many hats, Larry was the director of the flow cytometry laboratory. The flow cytometer counts and measures characteristics of cells. I began reviewing literature and discovered research on measuring the nuclear DNA content of cells. Most of the work had been done on fresh tissue, but I found a technique in which cells could be harvested from paraffin embedded tissue. With assistance from Sam and Nancy, the technologists, I reproduced the technique in our laboratory.

Since malignant cells have aberrant DNA content, my imagination ran rampant with the possibilities. In the histologic examination of tumors, a pathologist attempts to determine the cellular origin of the tumor, its benign or malignant classification and, if the latter, the tumor's growth rate and metastatic potential. Certain endocrine tumors of the adrenal, parathyroid, and thyroid glands and some cerebral astrocytomas frequently defy the benign versus malignant classification, which makes it very difficult to predict the behavior of the tumor and, therefore, the treatment indicated for the patient. Paraffin embedded tissues are kept and preserved indefinitely. My hope was that in retrospective studies of the patient's course and DNA analysis of their tumors, one might develop a nuclear thumbprint and predictor of a tumor's behavior.

My other university responsibilities included working in the anatomical pathology laboratory and making diagnoses on tissue samples. Often if a tumor's cellular origin eluded me, I held my decision overnight, placed it on a mental shelf, and prayed to be shown the answer. Without fail, the next morning the diagnosis was evident.

I also supervised pathology residents, and the residents performed the autopsies, so I was finally out of the morgue. In addition, I supervised pathology labs for medical students. After my experience in medical school, I was especially cognizant of treating the residents and students with kindness and respect.

By contract renewal time, my research was showing superb results, and Dr. Hensley was well vindicated in my hiring. I was promoted to Assistant Professor.

MY MARRIAGE

My personal evolution upset the equilibrium in my relationship with Dan, because Dan was heavily invested in taking care of me as he did his schizophrenic mother. When I was compromised by my surgeries and food addiction, I was predictable and manageable. As I led a more spiritually directed life, I had a new director, and it wasn't Dan.

Dan could rip me to shreds with his words, and he frequently derided me on my inadequacies as a mother and human being. We sought help through counseling, but it became apparent Dan had an infinite amount of rage directed toward me and much of it was related to his mother. Dan refused to acknowledge his anger, which made resolution impossible. He kept me with him by threatening to gain custody of the children. I thought so little of myself, I believed him. One day, after a particularly vicious verbal attack accompanied by shoving me around, the thought came to me, "Even I'm not that bad." I promptly sought legal counsel and served Dan papers. Dan refused to leave our home, and his behavior was so irrational and paranoid, I was concerned he might harm me or kidnap the children. I consulted our marriage counselor, and he validated my concerns and advised me to take precautions. I changed the locks on our home and temporarily put the children in hiding in a new daycare facility. Dan finally settled down. It was a rocky time for all of us. Sarah was five, and Jeffrey was three. With our divorce in the spring of 1986, we were awarded equal custody of the children.

ACADEMIC REWARDS

I worked three years with Larry, Sam, and Nancy, and we conducted numerous studies, which resulted in several published papers and abstracts. Dr. Hensley's replacement, Dr. Leech, called me the "Star of the Department."

In the fall of 1985, I received information calling for papers for several European meetings to be held in the summer of 1986. I thought, "All they can say is no," and proceeded to send my research to be considered for presentation. I told Larry of my plans, and he followed suit. We each had four papers or abstracts accepted for presentation in Stockholm, Vienna, and London, and these were to be given over a month's period. With our acceptances and the plan to visit flow cytometry laboratories in Rome, Edinburgh, and Amsterdam, we proposed our trip to Dr. Leech, who was pleased to provide departmental funding. With such obvious rewards, Dr. Leech hoped to generate other departmental members' enthusiasm for research and publication. Accompanied by Larry's wife, Madeline, we were off.

For me, the highlight of the trip was the art and not the conferences and laboratories, even though I found the professional activities interesting. We flew into Rome for a five-day stay in the middle of August. I basked in the flavor of the city with its fountains, architecture, and people. In Rome, my most profound experiences were viewing the Vatican and its Sistine Chapel and Michelangelo's scowling "Moses," found in the Church of St. Peter In Vinculis.

From Rome, we drove to Pisa and then the Renaissance mecca of Florence. Even a lifetime in Florence would be inadequate to fully savor her beauty, but over several days, trying to drink in as much as possible, I took the following tour.

In the Piazza Della Signoria, I viewed the beauty and anguish of the "Rape of the Sabine Women." From the Piazza, I entered the Palazzo Vecchio, the old residence of the Medici family, with its sumptuous rooms and views of the city. I especially enjoyed the lush, full-figured women lining its walls. They made me feel more welcome than the rail-thin beauties in the teeming streets below. Returning to the Piazza, I entered the Uffizi Gallery, with its marvelous Titians, Raphaels, and Botticellis. Walking a few blocks from this banquet, I came upon the Piazza del Duomo, containing the exquisitely detailed Cathedral of Santa Maria del Fiore and the Baptistry of St. John the Baptist. Opposite the cathedral, I entered the museum of the Opera del Duomo, with its wonderful reliefs and sculptures, which include Donatello's delightful dancing cherubs and his ascetic "Magdalene." The museum is also the home of Michelangelo's inspired third Pieta, "The Pieta of the Cathedral," and the gold door panels by Lorenzo Ghiberti from the neighboring Baptistry.

A few blocks farther, I arrived at the Gallery of the Academy, containing Michelangelo's magnificent "David" and four "Prisoners," as well as many lovely statues by Lorenzo Bartolini. From there, I walked to the Church of San Lorenzo and the Medici Chapels, containing the Tomb of Giuliano and Lorenzo de Medici and Michelangelo's sculptures, "Night," "Day," "Dusk," and "Dawn." The Pitti Palace's Boboli Garden and Palatine Gallery completed my tour, with the latter containing sumptuous Raphaels, Reubens, and Titians. Florence's artistic feast fed my soul.

We drove from Florence to Venice. Though beautiful and charming, Venice was pale in comparison to Florence.

From Venice, we drove through the Alps and saw its farming villages, chalets, and flower-filled window boxes. We arrived in Vienna, presented our papers, then explored her museums, palaces, and churches. While there, I attended my first opera.

Next, we flew to Stockholm and presented our papers, which were well received, as were all our presentations. Before touring the city, we bought sweaters to brace ourselves against Sweden's September chill, then visited "Old Town." During Larry's fellowship, Larry and Madeline lived in Sweden for a year, so we rode the train into the country and visited Larry's former professor. Due to recent rains, the Swedes were out picking mushrooms, and the widowed professor prepared his gatherings for our sumptuous evening meal.

We then flew to London for a brief stop and presentations. With little time to explore London, I remember it most for its busy streets and packed subways. In the latter, I felt like a sardine. Fearing for my life, I prayed for adequate oxygen and a safe trip, because the system appeared antiquated and unstable. In my moving underground entombment, I vowed to God, if allowed to survive, this would be my last ride on the London subway.

From London, we headed to Edinburgh, driving north across the English countryside with its picturesque thatched-roof homes, stone fences, and verdant pastures with grazing sheep. After touring a Scottish laboratory and buying several woolens, we drove southward and took a ship to our final destination, Amsterdam.

In Amsterdam, after taking in another laboratory and meeting with a distinguished colleague, we had two days to explore.

My favorite jewel from that leg of the trip was the Van Gogh Museum, with its superb depiction of the progression of Van Gogh's art and, unfortunately, also his madness. (*Years later, after Billy had not spoken to me for several years, he revealed, during our communication hiatus, he too had traveled to Amsterdam and been equally moved by the Van Gogh Museum. I was amazed by the synchronicity of our museum visits, which spoke to me of our deep resonance that surface emotions could not eradicate.*)

After a month, exhausted but immeasurably enriched, Larry, Madeline, and I returned home.

A PERMANENT CHANGE

At this point in my career, I received seventeen journals each month and had five four-drawer file cabinets filled with collated data on the field of pathology and disease. I realized I could generate and publish an endless array of papers, which might be of questionable benefit to humanity, for I had begun to suspect that my hope to develop a nuclear thumbprint and predictor of a tumor's behavior was not possible with the state of the available instrumentation. I was used up, depressed, and disillusioned with academia and the practice of pathology. Besides, in my spiritual journey, I realized that in pathology I was dealing with the wrong end of the life cycle—disease and death—instead of life and health.

As I peered through the microscope and diagnosed diseases that are considered to be "idiopathic" or of unknown origin, I agreed intellectually and intuitively with the writings of Louise Hay and Drs. Siegel, Jampolsky, and Cousins. They believe that when we internalize toxic substances, thoughts, and emotions, we create dis-eases in our bodies, including cancer. I also agreed with their premise that if we release these toxic thoughts, emotions, and behaviors and replaced them with positive, loving, life-affirming ones, we can heal our bodies, minds, and spirits. As these authors, I had also come to believe in the healing power of prayer and living a God-centered life.

During this time, Bob reported to me that Billy, at seventeen, had wrecked two cars and was drinking heavily. Bob and Molly were seeking help for Billy in an outpatient alcohol treatment facility and wanted me involved. I met with Jackie, Billy's counselor. Besides information and concerns for Billy, I discussed with her my depression and work stress. After listening to excerpts of my fast-paced, exhausting lifestyle, she asked, "From what are you running?" Immediately, I saw a wall of water, which I knew to be tears. I was afraid that if I stopped moving I would drown. Jackie recommended I go to codependency treatment. Because I knew treatment centers had family weeks, in hopes my son might get some help, I codependently agreed. Unknown to me, my life was to be permanently changed.

I entered a treatment center in the foothills outside Tucson, Arizona. The admitting physician and the first person I met was a neurosurgeon who no longer practiced neurosurgery. What a concept. I didn't have to practice pathology for the rest of my life. The thought had never before seriously taken root in my brain.

In my thirty days of treatment, I saw people express pain, anger, and deep hidden thoughts and deeds. After my childhood spankings, I cried only in secret, for I had long mastered the art of showing no emotion. While there, I cried to the depth of my being and even allowed others to hold me during the process. After my first day of such an experience, I felt a coat of armor clank to my feet. While there, I inventoried and shared every part of my life and its associated feelings.

I resisted asking my parents to family week but, when the counselors insisted and my parents agreed, my first conscious thought was, "Good, now the secrets will come out." This thought was accompanied by a visual image of Pandora's box opening, but Pandora didn't reveal her secrets so quickly. At that time, I suspect I was unprepared for its contents.

My parents and Billy arrived all ready to fix me. They got a rude awakening when it was disclosed they might have to look at themselves. The healing and unity I saw occur in other families did not happen in mine. In these family treatment settings, there is a process called "knee-to-knee," in which each family member confronts the designated "patient" about their behaviors, and the patient responds in kind. After exchanging the negative and positive information about the other person, the process of forgiveness and reconciliation usually occurs. When my turn came with my father, I could only cry. I knew something deep and black had happened between us, but I had no memory. I could not forgive him, because I didn't know for what he needed forgiveness. The answers were to come later. After that session, my father stormed off and left treatment early, taking with him my mother and son. I was estranged from my parents for three years and, after Billy graduated from high school the following spring, he cut off communication with me for more than seven years.

Interestingly enough, among the other families at treatment, the parent my father bonded with most was a man who, in the same session, was confronted on his sexual abuse of his daughter. That parent also left early.

I returned home and to my faculty position at the university. I knew I needed to leave my practice in pathology but had no idea where to go. I was terrified and certain I would become a bag lady. I spent nights on my bedroom floor crying and praying for the knowledge of God's will for me.

There is a story of a man stranded on an iceberg in the Arctic Ocean and praying for rescue. An Eskimo came by in a boat, and the fellow said, "Never mind God, I have it covered."

Well, I was praying on my iceberg.

One work day at noon, I took my lunch to the small park in front of the hospital. As I sat on the park bench, one of my former pathology residents, Willis, walked by, and we began to talk. I knew Willis had left the pathology program, and I asked where he was working? Willis was training in psychiatry at the state mental hospital in Norman.

After our fifteen-minute conversation, I knew I was to apply for a residency position in the same program. I knew Willis was my Eskimo, but unlike the man in the story, I remembered to thank God for my rescue.

WORK HIATUS

To the surprise and dismay of many of my colleagues, I left my pathology practice on December 31, 1986. My psychiatry residency began July 1, 1987 and, with a lot of prayer, I hoped to stretch my funds to cover a desperately needed six months of rest, soul searching, and emotional recalibration.

One of the first things I did in that six months was take a trip to Austin and attend a Louise Hay workshop. There, in a room with over a hundred participants, many of whom had AIDS or cancer, I saw this beautiful woman, radiant with light, tell how love for oneself and others could heal our bodies, souls, and the planet. I knew she was right and so was my decision to go into psychiatry.

I began to put my house in order and proceeded to pare down my lifestyle to live on a resident's salary. I sold many of my beautiful·furnishings, and the revenue filled my coffers a bit. With the stricken economy and deflated prices, I bought a modest but lovely home. After moving, I carefully painted each room. My new home was spacious and filled with light, but my mountain of boxes containing pathology books and files were a dark presence in the garage. One day, I became overwhelmed with the need to shed my old life and ceremoniously placed the boxes at the curb for trash pickup. In their absence, I felt a burden lift.

I was peaceful, content, and enjoying Jeffrey and Sarah, who were with me on alternating weeks. Billy, with his busy senior schedule, occasionally came to visit. I desperately wanted to connect with him, but his world was not accessible to me.

During this period, I sought to plumb myself to a greater depth. As I had the previous seven years, I prayed for God's will to be revealed in my life, spent much time in quiet meditation, and trusted my intuition as a guide by which to navigate.

Over the preceding one to two years, I again began to count calories, lose weight, and become more restrictive in my food intake. I was back to a size six. I also felt led by my body's intuition to follow a vegetarian lifestyle. Although nourishment without the consumption of flesh foods promotes health, the rigidity with which I pursued my dietary intake over the next five years was far from healthy.

Prior to leaving Pathology, my body longed to move and exercise, but I was mystified about how to begin. While on a visit to the Mayo Clinic to screen and select tissue blocks for a study on brain tumors, I was preparing for work one morning and watching a television exercise program. The woman was stretching and moving as my body longed to do. She was demonstrating the postures of Hatha Yoga. I promptly ordered her book and began my daily practice, which continues, although at times interrupted, to this day.

My yoga practice was particularly important for me during my work hiatus. Then and now it enhances my emotional well-being, quiets my mind, and enables me to tune in to my body and spirit. I have learned to trust my inner knowing, especially when it comes to me during times of meditation or yoga.

During this period, I also continued to strive to empty my internal vessel of defective traits of character, especially those causing me much discomfort or pain, such as pride, ego, fear, and anger. However, as in many of life's undertakings, that process is similar to water wearing away stone. Much time is required.

I worked to cleanse my body with proper exercise and nutrition, my spirit through prayer and meditation, and my mind with new thoughts and therefore new emotions and behaviors. As we align ourselves with God, I believe our minds and bodies act like radio receivers of positive vibrational energy from the Universal Divine. As we collect and channel this energy, we transmit it to those about us and to the world at large. I strove to be a better channel through which God could work.

THE NAVAJO RESERVATION

Sarah is Navajo and was six at the time. In hopes she might feel some connection to her Native-American heritage, I took her and Jeffrey to the Navajo Reservation. I don't know if our trip to Arizona accomplished that goal for her, but it certainly enriched my life.

In early June, the children and I embarked on a road trip which took us west on 1-40 through Amarillo and Albuquerque, then on to Gallup. From Gallup, we went northwest and entered the reservation. Our first stop was Window Rock, Arizona, the Navajo tribal headquarters. After the children had played around and through the rocks for which the town was named, we proceeded northwest across the reservation to Kayenta. The drive took us by exquisite outcroppings of wind- and water-chiseled red sandstone and Navajo hogans, with central smoke vents and doors facing east. With the help of their dogs, Navajo women, in traditional dress, were tending flocks of sheep. Except for a few tourists, Sarah saw only individuals with skin and hair similar to hers.

For several days, we stayed in the Anasazi Inn, south of Kayenta, located on the rim of Tsegi Canyon. Around the inn, Sarah and Jeffrey climbed rocks and played with Navajo children. The children and I explored the sights, which included walking the trails of the Navajo National Monument and the steep descent to the Anasazi ruins of Betatakin.

One day, the children stayed in the home of a park ranger and relative of R.C. Gorman, while I took an eight-mile horseback ride into the canyon and the Anasazi ruins of Keet Seel. The trail down into the canyon was perilous, but the horses were sure footed. Being afraid of heights, I just prayed and held on. Once in the canyon, a German anesthesiologist and I were allowed to give free rein to our horses and run them the canyon's gamut. The wind, sun, and ride were glorious. We reached the ruins, which like those of Betatakin, were located in a wind-carved arched recess of a cliff. We respectfully walked among the ancient dwellings and were amazed by their previous inhabitants' ingenuity and the tiny spaces in which they had resided. One could almost feel their presence and hear the songs of the old souls.

After a brown bag lunch, we returned back through the canyon and ascended the canyon wall. Bow-legged and walking slowly, I collected the children, who had baked and decorated a cake and thoroughly enjoyed their day.

One day at the inn, I observed a Native man, carrying a five-gallon container of water with a hand-held nozzle. He religiously sprayed a patch of green grass, an act not too dissimilar I suspect from the method his ancestors used to water their crops of corn, beans, and squash.

Other days, we toured the Valley of the Gods and Monument Valley and, in the latter, we toured by horseback, with Jeffrey riding with me and Sarah on a slow horse. I was deeply drawn to the beauty of the land's various hues of red and its powerful energy. After several days, we headed home going through Shiprock, Farmington, Taos, then southeast to Tucumcari, and on to Oklahoma City.

On returning home, the reservation and its energy called me, and I felt compelled to return before my psychiatry residency began. With the children at their father's for a week, I again drove to the reservation. With heightened sensitivity, I revisited the Navajo National Monument and spent hours sitting on red sandstone, soaking in the sun and the earth's vibrations.

On my first trip, I met a young Navajo woman, who offered me the use of her family's ceremonial hogan. During my second visit, I availed myself, for a night, of her generosity. The circular hogan's walls were constructed of rough hewn wood. Alone, I lay on a pallet of blankets spread on the earthen floor and peered at the stars through the smoke hole. As I slept cradled in the womb of Mother Earth, I felt one with the ancients.

Returning to Monument Valley, astride a horse and accompanied only by a guide, I ran the valley's length. The exhilarating experience was interrupted only by stops to drink in the view.

I drove the winding roads in the Valley of the Gods and, by automobile, made the sharp ascent to a plateau overlook. My being was filled and resonated with the energy of the red stone carved by nature's chisel.

With a full and peaceful soul, I returned home to begin my life's next phase.

CHAPTER SEVEN

Psychiatry Residency: The Secrets Unravel

♀

In July of 1987, I began my three-year psychiatry residency at Central State Psychiatric Hospital in Norman, Oklahoma. On my first day of residency, again the staff began to pimp us on Psychiatry Board Examinations. At that moment, I declared I'd had enough. I wasn't doing this again. I'd been tested from one end of the spectrum to the other and, at age forty, I refused to spend another three years with Boards casting a pall over my life. With all of my licenses and previous Board examinations, I knew that after my three years of residency I would be eligible for the Boards in psychiatry and could practice in that field, and that was good enough for me.

My first residency year was on an acute care ward. With moderate supervision, the residents evaluated and treated all admissions. The patients included the severely suicidal, homicidal, and psychotic. It was a stressful but invaluable experience. I learned to treat psychotic individuals with schizophrenia and bipolar disorder (manic-depressive disorder) in towering rages, both of

which, for their own safety, often required being confined to pad-
ded rooms. Locked in their own worlds, they screamed, talked
wildly, and sometimes stripped themselves naked, ate their own
feces, and urinated and smeared feces on the walls. With response to medication, I saw the same individuals become totally
lovable and endearing.

I heard horrifying stories of mental, physical, and sexual
abuse, which resulted in post-traumatic-stress disorder and, in
the most severe cases, multiple personality disorder (dissociative
identity disorder). I saw individuals with post-traumatic-stress
disorder and multiple personality disorder misdiagnosed as
schizophrenics, because their flashbacks were mistaken for hal-
lucinations, and their different personalities or regressed states
were thought to be evidence of psychosis.

I also saw hallucinating alcoholics and drug addicts misdiagnosed as schizophrenics and manic-depressives, medicated, and
shuffled off to psychiatric wards, with their addictions and alcoholism left untreated.

Beginning in my first year and continuing throughout my
residency, I worked with Karen, who had been satanically
abused by parents, grandparents, aunts, and uncles. Karen
had multiple personality disorder. Her compartmentalized
trauma memory took the form of many alters, which included children and adult males and females. As Karen began to
trust and feel safe with me, her various alters revealed themselves, and she retrieved their various packets of memory.
Karen's memory recall was necessary for her to integrate the
information and eventually integrate her personalities into a
functional whole.

During Karen's therapy, I met her grandfather. He seemed like a venerable old gentleman but, as her memory unfolded, she discovered he headed the satanic cult and was one of her primary perpetrators. In retrospect, I find it interesting that Karen was reared in the same area from which my parents issued and, though seemingly unrelated, her grandfather's surname was the same as my maiden name.

In making rounds on my patients, rather than having them brought to me, I frequently visited them in the communal areas on the ward. My fondest memory in residency is of such a day. I was standing and talking to several patients seated at a table, all of whom were in various stages of recovering from psychotic episodes. One of my patients stood and gently took my arm and moved me aside because, unknown to me, another patient was preparing to pour a Coke on my head. I felt very touched and tended.

Since there were several residents, our call schedule was not overly rigorous. However, on call nights with a full moon, I prayed and held on because those nights were always busy. When on call, the residents were available to the needs of more than three hundred patients. In addition, we were required to perform histories and physicals on any emergency admissions, so my interaction with patients far exceeded those for whose care I was directly responsible.

An event was related to me which revealed that I cannot predict what will be significant in my interaction with a patient and should therefore consider any patient contact as a therapeutic event. One night, a psychotic Mr. Jones, for want of a better name, was brought to the hospital emergency admitting area. He told the staff he would only talk to Dr. Bowlby or Dr. Johnson. I had no recollection of having treated this patient, but obviously whatever time we had spent together was important to him. Until then, I had the illusion my helping a patient was secondary to the amount of time and energy I expended with them in doing "quality therapy." Mr. Jones taught me any time I spend with a person is important and to be attentive and emotionally present, no matter how brief our encounter, because I never know when what I might say is important to a Mr. Jones.

HAPPILY EVER AFTER

During this first year of residency, though binge free, I continued to severely restrict my food and maintain a rail-thin body. I began to date Bill, a police officer and member of one of my spiritual groups. After having two abstract intellectual marriages with educated men, I decided an earthbound man might be more emotionally available. Although he was infatuated with me and I enjoyed his attention, I was not overly attracted to Bill. We dated for several months, and I intended to break up with him but ignored my intuition and became sexually involved. He proposed. Never before having experienced such sexual passion, I interpreted it as love and, in the summer of 1988, I again allowed myself to walk down the aisle. I was nothing if not persistent in my pursuit of "happily ever after."

In the marriage transition, I was drawn to simplify my life and release all attachment to objects, for I realized I didn't own the objects, they owned me. By this time in my life, my security and identity were based on God and not on my home's furnishings . Wanting to start my life anew, I sold my home and its contents, and Jeffrey, Sarah, and I moved into Bill's home. We attempted to settle in as a family and, with my money and some from a wedding gift from Bill's mother, we bought furnishings that were "ours."

I always seem to find men, or they find me, who need financing, and Bill was no exception. After the wedding, to demonstrate my commitment to the relationship and using the revenue generated from the sale of my home and furniture, I wrote checks expunging Bill's debt burden.

My income far exceeded Bill's, which was a hallmark for the men in my life. In February of 1989, at Bill's prompting, we became involved in a business venture. Since my work took all of my energy, Bill was to manage the business.

During this period, I had the vision of a six-year-old child sitting on a cellar door in an attempt to keep it closed, but being attacked on all sides by predators, she had to get off the door to protect herself. Unguarded, she feared the door would fly open.

By May, the business had failed. I felt financially raped, was severely depressed, and planned suicide. One day, I looked into Jeffrey's innocent six-year-old face. I had been told the suicide of a parent was the greatest trauma one could perpetrate on a child. I knew I had to get help or die.

TRAUMA MEMORY

I had been in therapy for years. Since codependency treatment, I knew I was sexually abused as a child. For trauma memory retrieval, I had done some "inner child" work, but I was able to access only a part of one memory. In this memory, I saw myself at age five, nude, with clothes dangling above my head, hiding inside a dark closet. Light streamed through the partially open closet door and, as I peered out, I saw my father's bare feet and hairy legs. I could advance no further in the memory. I was stuck.

As "luck"—God—would have it, my patient Karen had just returned from an inpatient sexual trauma treatment center in Los Lumas, New Mexico. I saw that she had improved. With my own suicide imminent, perhaps the treatment center could help me?

I told my residency supervisor of the dire nature of my depression. Within twenty-four hours of looking into Jeffrey's face, my moment of reckoning, I boarded a plane bound for New Mexico. As I said goodbye to Bill, I knew I was going to the center of my being, and my life would never again be the same.

The treatment center was in a relaxed, rural setting and consisted of white-washed buildings, patios, courtyards, and walking trails. I was greeted by a warm, nurturing staff, and I felt safe.

In the first week, I had a one-and-a-half-hour flashback. In a regressed state, I relived the trauma of a satanic cult ritual which occurred in my parents' barn when I was three to four years old. I screamed, groaned, and cried. I saw the carcass of a cow, with her belly splayed and exuding her intestines. I saw my mother's and my father's nude bodies covered with blood. As my father walked toward me holding a bloody knife, I heard my mother scream, "Paul, kill her." In my regressed state, my roommates and Karen, who had returned to treatment, touched, stroked, and soothed me. Their presence, especially Karen's, assured me I would survive. I had talked Karen through similar episodes, and I knew she hadn't gone permanently insane, so perhaps I wouldn't either.

The night after the flashback, as I walked across the courtyard, it was as if there was a cosmic explosion of my subconscious mind. Like a kaleidoscope, I saw fragments of memory flying out into the starlit New Mexico sky.

During my thirty days of inpatient treatment, I retrieved many memories. In any order and from every direction, they came in fragments, segments, and entire movie reels. Memories came in the form of pictures, smells, sounds, tastes, and crawling sensations on my skin. As they flooded through me, I rapidly journaled to capture each fragment before it flew from my mind, for they held the puzzle pieces to my life.

The experience boggled my mind. Had I not been in treatment with trained personnel who validated my reality, I would have interpreted my experience as a psychotic episode. Other patients also experienced similar memories, and the therapists, also trauma survivors, shared their personal experiences. I was not alone, and I was not insane. As unbelievable as the memories appeared and in the face of society's denial, people do perpetrate bizarre atrocities upon others. This is my reality and that of countless others.

To survive as the waves of agony swept through me, I prayed and held onto God. Through my remembering, doubled over in pain, I cried to the depth of my being. At other times, I spilled over with fury in directed anger work on pillows, beds, and couches. I felt like a tornado had ripped through my subconscious mind, exploding everything that had been neatly filed, stacked, and forgotten.

As I remembered my childhood, its reality became integrated into my being, and that integrated information is what I now share.

On the farm where we lived until I was three or four was a large wood-frame hay barn. Many things happened in that barn.

One day, while I played with kittens in the hay, the sun shone through the barn door. Suddenly, there appeared sun-framed figures of my father and another man. My father held me on the dirty floor while the man raped me.

There was the evening my mother sent me to the barn to fetch my father for supper. He took off my shorts and underpants. I sat bewildered and uncomfortable with my bare bottom on a prickly hay bale while my father performed oral sex on me and masturbated himself.

There was the night the barn contained many robed people. I saw a dead man, with a gaping abdomen and his bloody organs intertwined with snakes. My father stood me between the man's legs. With my nude body leaning toward the man's eviscerated bowel, my father anally raped me. The onlookers reveled in Satan's power. My father headed the cult.

Some of my mother's "punishments" also occurred in the barn. For a long-forgotten infraction, she placed me and a snake in a wooden cage. To be free of its horror, I attempted to poke the snake's head through the cage slats, but the openings were too small.

Another day my mother locked me naked in the barn's feed room. In terror, I huddled in a corner and watched the rats. I was afraid they would eat me.

The dark and isolated house on that farm was no safer than the barn. I remember it only in black and white.

I recall being in my crib in a dark room, knowing I was totally alone and no one would ever come to pick me up or love me. I was sad to my marrow.

In that crib, I saw my mother and felt the sharp stab of an ice pick as it glanced off my ribs. She wanted me dead. Three years before I was born, my mother birthed a daughter. My sister supposedly died of "heart trouble." I continue to wonder if my mother killed her?

In my first year, I was placed on the kitchen floor and tied to a chair leg. Three snakes also occupied the floor. I was quiet and bewildered. They were my playfellows, a form of conditioning for rituals, because the cult frequently used ceremonial serpents.

Many things happened in that kitchen. My mother was adamant I should eat everything on my plate, and my failure to do so brought swift reprisals. Once, as a consequence for not eating my dinner, my mother forced my face into a plate of dog excrement. Another time, she fried a rat and made me eat it.

I could only have my dessert if I cleaned my plate, and I loved cookies. I once hid cookies and stole out to eat them without finishing my meal. I was apprehended by my mother and locked in a wooden box behind the house. The box was filled with nonpoisonous snakes used in rituals. I silently screamed but lay stone-still, because I knew any sound or movement would agitate the snakes, and I abhorred feeling them slither on my skin. When my mother finally removed the lid from the box, I ached to be held and comforted, but comfort never came.

On several occasions, I was tied spread-eagled on the kitchen floor. Once, my mother criss-crossed my abdomen with cuts by a butcher knife and, with relish, licked her blood-covered fingers. Another time, with her fingers, she clamped the head of a snake, rubbed the snake on my body, then placed its head in my vagina. All the while she crooned, "He loves you. He loves you." Afterwards, she masturbated herself with the snake. I suspect my mother had sustained similar childhood abuse.

Poisonous snakes were also used in the rituals. The cobra was kept in a covered basket. (*My father was in the Philippines during World War II, which I suspect was the origin of the cobra.*) My bedroom was lonely and dark, with only a single window next to my twin bed. One day the basket was placed beside my bed. I am sure with suicidal intent, I released the cobra. Initially, as I had been taught, I calmed the serpent by stroking its back. Later, the cobra fanned. In memory, I saw my child-self stone-still and silent, looking into the cobra's eyes. I knew with one move I would die. I decided to live another day. My father later returned the snake to its basket.

My mother was subject to violent fits of rage, and she was very jealous of my father's "affection" for me. She once held my hand and allowed a rattlesnake to bite me. She told my father I had been playing with it. A doctor was not called. How could it be explained? As I lay on my bed in my dark bedroom, I was violently ill and near death.

Another time, my mother attempted to drown me in a creek. As I struggled and gasped for air, my father stopped her.

One night from my bed, I heard my mother crying and my father hollering. I knew he was beating her. In hopes he would stop, I pretended to be thirsty and went to ask for a drink of water. He dragged me onto the bed. While raping me, he said to her, "She can do it better than you." I was a codependent at age three.

For years to come my father repeated a ritual. With his fingers, he clamped the head of a snake, used the snake's head like a penis in my vagina, and masturbated himself. When I was three, my father once took me to my parents' bedroom. In separate containers, he had the cobra and rattlesnake. He used them on me in that order. I was terrified. Attempting to get out, my dissociated spirit hovered above the window. I could see the cobra fanned in the corner and my father on the bed with me and the other snake. I was horrified with the thought that the cobra might kill him while he used the rattlesnake on me, and if he died, so would I.

(*After retrieving my memories, I understood a dream that repeated itself throughout my life: As a child, to get to my elementary school, I had to walk across the playground. In my dream, the playground was covered by black snakes. To access the school, I had to carefully step between coiled serpents.*)

A few months before we moved from that farm, my brother, John Paul, was born. While my mother was in the hospital, a nice lady came to care for me. She cooked a wonderful breakfast, bacon and eggs.

When I was four, my family and I moved to the farm where my parents still reside. I got older. Nothing changed.

At age five, I played house on the back porch. One day, unaware of danger, I sang, chattered, and played with my dolls and dishes. My father came from behind and dragged me into their bed. He attempted to rape me. I struggled. He violently separated my legs and dislocated my right hip. Afterwards, I ceased playing and became silent and vigilant.

On a moonlit night, I was taken from my bed to a clearing on the farm, placed on an altar, and circled by chanting, dark-robed figures. My curly long blonde hair cascaded over the edge of the altar. My father carried a subdued cobra limp between his hands and placed it on me. The cobra fanned. As my body lay motionless, my spirit soared out to a nearby tree, then into the sky. Because I survived the test, the cult believed I had sacred powers and was indeed "Satan's Daughter."

When I was attempting to learn my multiplication tables, my mother made me join her as she milked in the dairy barn. As I struggled with the numbers, she became angered, stripped me of my clothes, tied me spread-eagled on the cold dirty concrete, and placed spiders on my stomach.

Before the age of ten, I was dressed in a white lace dress and veil. Surrounded by the cult, I walked down an aisle on my father's arm and was wed. I became the "Bride of Satan." (*No wonder within two weeks after each set of marriage vows, I was ready for a divorce.*)

As I grew and developed, my father continued to molest me with snakes. He did it out-of-doors, in the granary, and in my bedroom.

Sometimes, as punishment, I was locked nude in the granary, where the cobra and a boa constrictor were kept. They ate rats. Once I looked with terror at a mound of yellow grain as the cobra slid toward me. Another time, I watched and listened as my father unbuckled his belt and unzipped his pants, as he prepared to rape me.

The boa constrictor and I grew up together. When I had my first memory of it, I only saw flashes of its head with its serrated teeth pointing toward its stomach. I promptly consulted a text to validate the accuracy of my memory. I remembered correctly.

Working the night shift at a local factory, my father always returned home in the middle of the night. In the summer through the window opened to catch a cooling breeze, I would hear the bang of the barn screen door and watch, by moonlight, as he headed toward the house, carrying two gunnysacks. I knew the ritual well. He would lay the big lug of a boa constrictor by me on the bed. As he vaginally used the black snake on me to simulate a penis, he masturbated himself.

During the abuse, I prided myself on being able to control my emotions. For my face had mastered the look of a blank slate. But with my development, my father took maniacal pleasure in arousing my body, and I felt betrayed by my body's response and was engulfed with shame.

At thirteen, I was forced to lay in a cut hayfield by an idling tractor. On the dirt, rocks, and stubbles, my father anally, then orally raped me. Inside, I screamed, "Why is he doing this? Can't he see how ugly I am?" I knew he loved beautiful women. I had cut my hair to short brown stumps, gained weight, and had the pimples of adolescence.

At various times in my preteens and early teens, I was forced to perform oral sex on my mother or her mother. Their bodies were so vile to me, I despised the shape, hair, and smell of my developing woman's body.

When I was sixteen, my father came to collect me from a school function. I wore a white dress that exposed the lovely shape of my breasts and waist. He drove me to a motel and anally raped me. Afterwards, in a dissociated state, I observed myself washing the blood and feces from my body, and I knew that I would remember nothing the next morning. I was very practiced in forgetting. Indeed, the next morning, I dressed for school, made straight A's, and continued in my trance, an automaton. I was locked in the silence of my forgotten memories.

As a little girl, I spent hours arranging my dolls perfectly on my bed. They were dressed perfectly, perfectly in order, and perfectly still. I did not play. I invented the dolls' lives, and their lives became mine. The world as I knew it did not exist.

Because of my sexual trauma, I developed self-abusive, obsessive-compulsive behaviors. For disfigurement, I frequently cut my hair to short stubs or mutilated my skin. In my eating disorder, I vacillated from anorexia to compulsive overeating. In my anorexic phase, I stripped my body of all vestiges of womanness. I had control over my breasts, hips, and thighs. I could make them disappear, and I knew my perpetrators liked my feminine curves. In my compulsive overeating phase, food was an anesthetic, numbing my pain. With overeating, my excess weight became a cloak from the world, providing a buffer from sexual attention and predators. I felt strong. My body's size said, "I am big. You can't hurt me!" Such are the boasts of a frightened child.

Eating or not eating, dissociating, and forgetting were how I survived. The beginning of the end of these behaviors began during my thirty days in New Mexico. I left treatment with my old life shattered. God was my only remaining support.

CHAPTER EIGHT

North to Alaska

♀

I BELIEVE EVERYTHING IS IN DIVINE RIGHT ORDER, but I don't always like or understand the order. I now know God had prepared me in my spiritual journey to weather the storm of my reality, and my reliance on God safely bore me through its remembering.

Departing from treatment, I flew to Oklahoma City and arrived in a torrential downpour. Bill met me at the airport and took me to my car. While away, I took a hard look at my relationship with Bill and his financial exploitation of me. I was repulsed by the idea of living in his home. It felt dirty and unsafe. Besides, I was unsure if I could ever again allow a man to touch me.

Emotionally fractured and frightened, I drove my car through the rain, looking for a place to stay. As I searched for a motel, I saw people in square dancing attire going in and out of buildings. Obviously, a square dancing convention was being held. My parents were square dancing enthusiasts and often attended such gatherings. Terrorized by the thought of seeing them, I prayed, attempted to remain rational, and finally found a room for the night.

Emotionally raw, I felt as if my skin had been ripped off. I knew that I was starting my life anew and that I needed to create a nurturing environment for myself in which I could heal. The next day I rented a white-walled apartment, occupied by new furniture. Everything that surrounded me had to feel safe and clean. I wanted nothing used by another human. I felt like a burn victim wrapped in sterile gauze.

Shortly after settling in my apartment, I wrote my parents that I had just returned from incest treatment and told them, "A child doesn't forget. I remember everything. Do not write or contact me again."

I had a year remaining in my psychiatry residency and was barely able to function. To survive emotionally and financially, I had to complete my training. Before returning to work, I told my supervisors and fellow residents of my experience and asked for their understanding and support, which they readily provided.

On returning to work, I struggled to cope with my day-to-day existence and had nothing left for Sarah and Jeffrey. As Billy before them, Jeffrey and Sarah went to live with their father. For years, I struggled with the pain of the time lost with them and the guilt of feeling like an "unfit mother."

I continued to have frequent memories through the year following treatment and could identify when a new memory was surfacing, because the memory was always preceded by an intense compulsion to binge and commit suicide. My belief in reincarnation kept me alive. Believing we incarnate on the planet to be taught spiritual lessons, I sure wanted to learn the lessons of this lifetime because I didn't want to repeat this sucker again. To heal emotionally, I knew that I must feel the pain and allow the memories to surface, and that no matter what, I must not binge or hurt myself.

After I was home a few weeks, I began to have recurrent intense right hip pain, which became so excruciating Bill took me to a hospital emergency room. There followed a five-day hospitalization with tests and x-rays. The orthopedist concluded I had degenerative changes of the spine, but I knew I had experienced and extruded the body memory, stored at a cellular level, of my childhood rape and hip dislocation.

That year the memories and feelings came through like freight trains. With each new memory, I cried and convulsed agonizing sounds from the depth of my being. I found when I allowed the memory to come, like the aftermath of a freight train, my soul was quiet.

During my recovery, I realized that my trauma was like a non-replenishing well of pain and, each time I felt the pain and cried to the core of my being, the pain occupied less and less space within. Each segment of pain I felt and released did not have to be experienced again. I might feel other segments related to that piece of work, but work processed did not have to be repeated.

I also realized that all feelings come through the same channel or pipeline, and I was getting a long needed mega-Roto Rooter of the soul. As my channel was cleansed of negative feelings, peace, love, and joy began to take their place.

Through that year, I attended a weekly women's therapy group, which provided support and validation of my process. In addition, I knew various forms of body work could help cleanse my body of memories and negative emotions, so I found a Rolfer, Eric, who worked on my deep tissues for more than twenty sessions. Those who have been Rolfed know that Rolfing is not for the faint of heart.

Episodically that year, Bill and I tried to reconcile, but I had a recurrent dream of him lying in a bed with dirt and dried feces beneath it, which of course repelled me. Besides the dream, I intuitively knew Bill was not my life's partner, but I kept being drawn to him. Finally, I realized when he touched me his hands were like a magnet and resembled those of my father. In my therapy, I was told, "Sexual abuse of a child is the most powerful hypnotic known to humans." With the dots connected, the spell was broken.

On my filing for a divorce, Bill asked for alimony, which he did not receive, but his request was a glaring statement of his character.

In the meantime, I was approaching completion of my psychiatry residency. Before starting my training, I planned to open a private office in Oklahoma City and work with individuals recovering from eating disorders, alcoholism, and drug addiction. As graduation approached, I was drawn to look elsewhere, but where I didn't know.

One of my fellow residents returned from an Indian Health Service recruiting seminar and told me of the states in which jobs were available. I was intrigued. I respect and revere Native American people and feel a strong spiritual connection with them. Positions were available on the Navajo Reservation, and I thought Arizona would be my choice but, for the adventure, I decided to go through the interview process. I first visited a reservation in South Dakota, but the position wasn't a fit. In February of 1990, I interviewed in Alaska and was hooked. Looking like a "winter wonderland," Alaska's raw untamed beauty beckoned me, and I answered.

That summer, I traded my Pontiac sedan for a four-wheel-drive Toyota Forerunner and, with nine-year-old Sarah, I headed north. We were on the road for eleven days and camped in fields, on the roadside, and in parks. We fought mosquitoes and fatigue but not each other. Desiring sole proprietorship of Sarah's affection, Dan had long planted himself as a barrier between Sarah and me. But without his interference, Sarah and I laughed, played, enjoyed the adventure, and shared many tender moments.

Alaska felt safe. It was over four thousand miles from my parents and had no snakes. Continuing to shun the burden of objects, I settled into another furnished apartment. Then, Sarah and I continued our adventure and drove north from Anchorage. We drank in the sights of Mount McKinley, or "Denali" as the Alaskans call it. Driving through the park and from a distance, we saw bears and caribou. On returning to my new home, with tears, Sarah and I parted, and she returned to Oklahoma City for the school year.

On weekends, before the winter snows, I set out to explore Alaska by car. Driving south from Anchorage, I drove around the inlet and between majestic snowcapped mountains and on to Seward and Homer. Walking along Homer's shoreline, I collected energy-filled stones, which were so powerful I could not allow them in my bedroom. They kept me awake. Later, over winter's snowpacked roads, I made the same trip and saw more than forty eagles perched on Homer's spit, where the fishermen fed them daily.

(One can feel the energy of a rock, mountain, or another person because "matter as we know it is an illusion. What we see around

us are not solid rocks, towering trees, flowing rivers, and corporeal beings, each one different from all others. Behind those appearances are whirling masses of atoms. Even the atoms are an illusion," for atoms are composed of subatomic particles, which are whirling masses of energy. Behind the appearances of solid forms is "an ocean of energy manifesting itself through the atoms as rocks, trees, water, and human and animal bodies."[1]

In the fall, driving east from Anchorage, I went through Palmer and the gorgeous Matanuska Valley, ringed by sharp angular mountains. Until I saw the aspens turn, I was unaware of the many exquisite shades of yellow and gold. East of the Valley, I turned northeast and drove above the treeline and camped near the base of the breathtaking Alaska Range, replete with snow and glaciers. These magnificent mountains could have birthed the spires of European cathedrals. These megalithic peaks were like radio antennae, amplifiers, and transmitters. Their energy reverberated through me and filled every cell of my body.

On an eight degree day, I experienced my first Alaskan Thanksgiving. At noon, when I stepped outside to join friends for lunch, the air was so sharp that crystals formed in my nostrils. The sun was piercingly bright and shimmered on the hoarfrost that blanketed the trees. Alaska was radiantly dressed in her pristine splendor.

In my first Alaskan winter, I decided I must learn to ski, so I rented skis and trekked off to the mountains for a Saturday lesson. In Anchorage, at the winter solstice, the sun is above the horizon from 10:00 a.m. to 2:00 p.m. In the dark morning, as I ascended the designated mountain, a snowstorm set in. On my right was the white wall of the mountain, the road was white in front of me, to my left was a white drop-off, and my vision was obscured by the heavy snowfall. Now a less determined individual would have stopped their vehicle or found a way to turn around and go home. Not me. I didn't want the rough and rugged Alaskans to consider me a "sissy"—shades of medical school. I prayed and persevered to the lodge, which of course was closed due to the storm. I gratefully followed a snowplow back down the mountain and thanked God that my car and body were not to be found on the side of the mountain at spring thaw.

WORK—MY SALVATION

Though the magnificence of Alaska fed my soul and Jeffrey and Sarah visited at Christmas, my first Alaskan winter was long, dark, cold, lonely and forced me to reach deep within myself and walk close to God. I hurt, prayed, meditated, and worked. My patients were my salvation and, in helping them, I helped myself.

My position was as an outpatient staff psychiatrist at the Alaska Native Medical Center in Anchorage. Upon arrival, I was told that Native people would not participate in group therapy. In spite of that information, that winter I started my first weekly, long-term women's therapy group, which was designed to treat recovering addicts, alcoholics, and survivors of emotional, physical, and sexual abuse. I facilitated that group for four years. The numbers of women desiring treatment became so large, I began a second group and then a third. After five years, I had treated over one-hundred-and-forty women, with some women attending their group for more than two years. As they healed, so did I. They shared their reality, as I did mine. I did not do my own therapy in group, but I wanted the women to know no matter how deep their pain, I also had known, survived, and healed from such pain. I wanted them to know that no matter what their injuries, they could recover, and I was one of them.

I derived great joy watching these women blossom before my eyes. Their lights came on. Someone was home inside. Their steps quickened and, in their healing, they helped others.

The Alaska Native population has an extremely high incidence of alcoholism and sexual abuse, and at times, I felt overwhelmed by the numbers needing help. Often we do not act because we believe our efforts won't make a dent in the need, but one person can make a difference. We just have to roll up our sleeves and get to work. Our actions, like one stone thrown into a lake, form an ever-expanding circle of waves.

In the second year, I was made chairperson of the eleven member department and, on a weekly basis, I was the psychiatric liaison for two local inpatient alcohol and drug treatment centers. In Oklahoma, I frequently court committed to treatment alcoholics and addicts who were a danger to themselves or others. I found such a law also existed in Alaska and proceeded to do the same, especially committing pregnant alcoholic women who were endangering the health of their unborn children. To my surprise, the addiction treatment community became pleasantly excited, because I was the first person who had ever used the law.

OTHER LIVES

Throughout my time in Alaska, I daily prayed, meditated, and performed hatha yoga postures. I also regularly attended spiritual support groups and found a therapist for individual work.

I also continued my body work and had regular massages. In the summer of 1991, I found Jan who worked in greater depth with body energy and began a series of sessions with her. I had no preconceived notions of this work. In our first session, she instructed me in deep breathing exercises, and much to my surprise, the following occurred:

I began to see a raised cobra. I then realized I was viewing and simultaneously in the body of a six- or seven-year old boy. He was kneeling at his father's feet. His father, an Egyptian pharaoh, was cloaked in heavy robes, and on each side of his father and facing the child were fanned cobras. Well trained, the boy remained motionless even though his knees ached on the rough stone floor. Later, his father left and the two serpents were removed by handlers. The child, whose mother was a slave, was then free to move. I next saw him as he walked down an arched palace corridor. He was a strong, muscular, blonde young man and wore a garment resembling a short toga. Next, in formal attire and headdress, I saw him in a large ceremonial room, lit by torches, which were held by bearers. Behind him was a series of six to seven steps, at the top of which sat his enthroned father. In front of him was an altar, on which lay a beautiful maiden dressed in white. She had coal-black hair, and her head was circled by a gold band, which anteriorly bore the replica of a serpent.

The young man was a priest, and over his outstretched hands lay a relaxed cobra. The priest's mission was to place the soothed cobra on the girl. Her survival symbolized her sacredness and worthiness to become a priestess. The girl became frightened and startled the slumbering snake. With her death, the young man was ravaged with grief, for he had loved her. He blamed himself for being unable to sufficiently soothe the cobra. In anguish, he placed his hand in a basket containing an asp. Along with several live cobras, his body was placed in a stone sarcophagus. From the outside of the coffin, I, Self, viewed my body through the stone.

On my re-entering this lifetime, Jan said that while working on me she also had a vision of a cobra on my stomach.

After this past life recall, I understood one of the reasons for this incarnation and my satanic abuse. I, the pharaoh's son, could not forgive myself for being human, so in part, I chose this life-time as a punishment for the girl's death. I then knew one of my lessons for this lifetime was to forgive myself for being human. I was also relieved to know this lifetime was not a punishment for some karmic evil I had perpetrated.

It would be several years before I would have memories of other lifetimes.

MOUNTAIN-TOP PERCH

In the spring of 1992, I bought a home on a mountain, one of the Chugiak Range, east of Anchorage. The ceilings, walls, and floors of my home were lined with knotted wood, interrupted only by spacious windows across the west and south walls. Each morning, I arose, donned leotards, and did yoga from my mountain-top perch overlooking a panorama of the Cook Inlet, the Alaska Range, the mountain called "Sleeping Lady" and, on a clear day, I could see Denali.

From my home, I viewed sunsets with the most mesmerizing hues of pink and blue and, at night, the lights of Anchorage sparkled below me. From my kitchen window, I watched bull moose in rutting season and winter's cross-country skiers.

In my home, I continued to have little need for furniture. I slept on a floor pallet and surrounded myself with plants and high-energy Alaskan rocks. I was particularly drawn to the energy frequency of black stones with white striations. My mountain sanctuary provided a beautiful setting for the continued healing of my wounded and fractured spirit.

Since sixteen, I had struggled with my eating disorder. In the summer of 1992, I had been anorexic for years. It had been twelve years since I had eaten sugar, bread, a sandwich, or pizza. I broke. I could no longer diet, count calories, or weigh and measure me or my food. I felt like a clay pot that had been thrown against a wall and shattered into a thousand pieces. I was done.

For years, I prayed and asked God for help, but I wouldn't give God control of what or how I ate. I didn't trust God in that arena of my life. God could have control of all other aspects of my being but not my weight. Just a bit of incongruity there.

With my eating out of control, I was praying and, like a shipwreck, sinking fast. I was terrified of another massive weight gain. Ad nauseam, I had read diet and eating disorder books, but by "serendipity" through a friend I discovered the writings of Geneen Roth, which permanently changed my life. In Roth's books, I read of my body's divine wisdom and how my body intuitively knows what it needs to eat and what size it needs to be. What a concept. I read about eating only when I am hungry, stopping when full, and eating what sounds good. The concept was simple and a well-kept secret by the billion dollar diet industry. It also worked.

Though I trusted my intuition and inner knowing in all other areas of my life, I hadn't trusted it with my body's size or the foods I consumed. What a relief to trust God and my body's wisdom to guide me. With renewed hope, I ceremoniously cut up, then burned my measuring tape. My hips and thighs were on their own.

In the fall of 1992, I became intensely suicidal, and knew without help, I would soon die. All my life, I had battled depression but didn't know it. I thought what I felt was normal. I could only identify my feelings as depression when I became suicidal. Prior to beginning my spiritual journey in 1980, I was suicidal on a daily basis and didn't plan on shoes or tires wearing out.

After 1980, I continued to be suicidal on an infrequent basis. Again facing death and having done all the therapy any human could tolerate, I again became willing to give control to something outside of me and tried antidepressants. Prior to that time, I rigidly held to the notion that therapy or God could heal all emotional problems, but I was overlooking the obvious fact that God made medications available for human use. Thank goodness for myself and my patients, I was willing to change. For the first time in my life, my depression lifted, and I began to see the world through more joyful eyes. Happiness became commonplace. It was a miracle.

HOLIDAYS

Jeffrey and Sarah visited that Christmas and had a great time playing in the snow. I again rented skis and scheduled lessons, but the weather was frigid and miserably cold feet ended our Alpine careers.

The following February, I went for a week's holiday retreat in Hawaii with a group Jan had organized. There, I learned techniques to work with the body's energy, my own and others and, with a reprieve from the Alaskan winter, I luxuriated in the sun, ocean, and tropical terrain. Located in a rural setting, the retreat center served only vegetarian food and had a delightful 1960s feel. Nearby, the pebbled beach was accessible by descending a steep path and, on the beach, clothes were optional. I allowed myself to briefly experience nude bathing, and the sea felt marvelous on my bare skin. One morning, I ventured to the beach to meditate and was privileged to observe a blonde nude male, with the form of a Greek god, reverently perform Tai Chi.

On my last night at the center, a Native American man led a sweat. Fifteen of us wrapped in towels filed into the small lodge. In the dark, we were tightly seated around the tepee's perimeter. Water was sprinkled on hot stones located in the center, and outside a bonfire continued to heat stones, which were periodically passed inside and added to the stack. Sage was passed about the circle and, as each person received it, they offered a prayer. The sage circled and circled. The heat was intense, and the air scant. At first, I felt I must flee, but I held myself there. To tolerate the claustrophobic conditions, I focused on one point deep within myself and prayed. Going through the eye of the needle, my consciousness left the lodge. When the sweat was completed, we filed out. I hurriedly dressed and walked to the ocean's edge. As I leaned against a palm tree, the full moon shimmered across the water, the stars glistened, and my spirit soared.

MARRIED AGAIN

During my third year in Alaska, I met Chuck, a 5'2" burly Scotsman who worked as a surveyor and had lived in Alaska for twenty-five years. Chuck's home was a self-made log cabin located two hundred miles east of Anchorage. Chuck had reared five children, fished and hunted for food, and had many a tale to tell of his Bush life. I was fascinated and charmed.

For the fourth time, in the summer of 1993, I married, continuing my pursuit of home and family. After the marriage ceremony, I knew I was in trouble when Chuck turned to me and asked for money to buy his daughters' lunch. I had already bought our wedding rings, and I didn't even propose. The marriage and finances went downhill from there.

On weekends, Chuck and I drove to his homestead and, in doing so, we enjoyed seeing Anchorage in our rear-view mirrors. Chuck's cabin was definitely back to basics, but I loved it. We had electricity, propane for cooking, a wood stove for heat, and an outhouse for necessities. We had no indoor plumbing, and we hauled our water. Bathing often consisted of a dishpan of hot water, what one of my patients laughingly called a "bird bath." A tub of hot water was a prized commodity.

For winter night outhouse runs, I donned a coat and boots and kept a lookout for bears and moose. Even though I don't like synthetics, I was grateful for the styrofoam-lined seat, which was temperature neutral and prevented splinters. I was also grateful for the outhouse rules in which men were not allowed to urinate while standing, or the ice would be there for the next person who came to sit. On my way back to the house,

I often stopped and gazed into the clear starry sky and reveled in a breathtaking aurora borealis.

During summers at the homestead, I planted a garden, then waited and watched as the long Alaskan days worked their magic. Alaska is renowned for its large vegetables. Though mine did not obtain Alaska State Fair size, I relished the beauty and bounty of my cabbages, cauliflower, and broccoli. My garden also abounded in rhubarb.

In the fall, keeping an eye out for bears, I experienced the bliss of picking blueberries and low bush cranberries in the woods. When the winter came and the earth was snow-laden, I baked blueberry and cranberry muffins and pies, and my special concoction, blueberry-rhubarb pie. Each time I removed the steaming pastries from the oven or took a juicy bite, I remembered the lovely days spent on the hillsides and in the forest picking berries.

At the homestead in the winter, twenty below was common, and I enjoyed the exercise of stacking wood and stoking the fire. When performing these tasks, I felt powerful and self-sufficient.

At the homestead, I also spent long winter days sewing, quilting, and watching professional football and basketball games. With television close-ups, I enjoyed observing the players' athletic prowess, their personalities, and the psychodynamics of the game.

With winter's long visit in Alaska, I had ample time to enjoy these simple pleasures. Unlike Oklahoma's spring of daffodils and green grass, Alaska's "spring" consists of the beginnings of melting snow, newly visible highway pavement, and the return migration of birds that kept their feathers warm by wintering in southern climes.

The homestead cabin's north wall had three large windows that framed the distant snow-covered Wrangell-St. Elias Mountains, which could be viewed from every location in the house and were our constant mealtime companions. I relished this simple down-to-earth existence, which Chuck made possible, but as my children are fond of saying, "Mom, you don't have to marry them."

MORE CHANGE

After four-and-a-half years in Alaska, the Indian Health Service began to undergo major reformation, and the psychiatry department was in the process of expanding to forty employees. In addition to my administrative duties, I continued to facilitate groups and treat many patients on an individual basis. After going full steam since my arrival in Alaska, I was used up and ready for a change. In December of 1994, I resigned my position, sold my mountain-top retreat, and moved permanently to the Bush and my husband's cabin. I planned to do a little consultation work with the local Native American health clinic, but primarily I wanted to rest, regroup, pray, and be led into my work's next phase. Little did I suspect where I was about to be catapulted.

Living with Chuck twenty-four hours a day was an eye-opener. After Christmas that year, we left on what I now term "the vacation from hell." I thought we had planned a leisurely pace of doing "whatever," but mainly being together and relaxing in New Mexico and Arizona. A year earlier, in an economy move, I sold the Toyota and purchased a 1986 Suburban. On a frigid day, we drove south in the Suburban down the Alaskan-Canadian Highway. Once in the "Lower 48," as the Alaskans call it, we made our route through Washington and stopped in Idaho to spend several days with Chuck's mother, visit his friends and relatives, and buy a camping trailer.

From Idaho, we went to Wyoming and had a brief but delightful stay in Yellowstone. We journeyed on to Colorado and Kansas, then stopped in Oklahoma to spend a few very special days with Jeffrey and Sarah.

From Oklahoma, we drove to Arkansas to visit Chuck's friends, Don and Wanda, who had also become my friends. From Arkansas, we traveled on to Texas. Chuck's family issued from Texas and many remained to populate the countryside. In Texas, Chuck visited every relation he could locate. Apparently, I was just along for the ride, and my smile and congeniality wore very thin. Chuck loved to hear himself talk. With each unearthed relative or friend, he repeated the same tales that I was tired of hearing before we left Alaska. To say the least, I was not amused. After six weeks, I was exhausted by strangers, broke down in tears, and insisted on returning home to Alaska. After financing the trailer and trip, I was totally disgusted and too tired and homesick to spend the time I craved in New Mexico and Arizona.

My first two husbands, Bob and Dan, were emotionally unavailable and negated my worth as a human being. My third and fourth husbands, Bill and Chuck, affirmed me as a person, but I was their financier. Chuck had fallen on self-induced "hard times," and I was a sucker for a "fixer upper." Early in the marriage, as Bill before him, I helped Chuck clear his debt. After returning from our vacation, he wanted to get his survey business up and going and needed new equipment and a computer. Men seem to glorify in their computer toys. I often wonder if computers are like some sort of penile fixation, with men comparing who has the biggest, fastest, and newest?

Again, to show my commitment to the marriage, I made the cash outlay for Chuck's business, with the agreement that I would be reimbursed for my investment. In my gut, I knew I would never see the money again, and I didn't. Again, I felt financially raped.

On April 19, 1995, the Oklahoma City Murrah Federal Building was bombed, and I felt as though a bomb had exploded inside me. I had no respect for Chuck and was miserable in my marriage. During my yoga, I diligently prayed for God's guidance. Four times my inner voice said, "Go back to Oklahoma." I kept saying, "You've got to be kidding." I never planned to return and could think of other places I'd much rather live. The fifth time my inner voice came, it said, "I've already told you, you're not listening." Finally, I surrendered and began to make plans to return to Oklahoma, but I wanted to give Jeffrey and Sarah one last Alaskan summer. Also, in the preceding year, Billy had contacted me and was coming to spend two weeks with us that summer.

For years, Billy had harbored anger toward me for divorcing his father and for my subsequent marriages that also resulted in divorce. Except for a few occasions, Billy had not communicated with me since my codependency treatment and his exit with my parents. Over the years, I had ached to hear from him, but I was powerless over his decision. All I knew to do was pray, work on myself, and be ready when he contacted me. On the Thanksgiving before I left the Indian Health Service, the call came. Billy was living in Washington, D.C., and attending law school at George Washington University. Through that winter, we communicated by phone and mail, and I desperately wanted to give Billy an Alaskan adventure that summer.

With a heavy heart, I talked with Chuck. Our relationship was not working for him either, but he agreed to help me make the children's summer memorable.

Jeffrey and Sarah came a month before Billy's scheduled visit. They were unaccustomed to the isolation of the homestead. Our closest neighbor was a mile away, and I didn't know them. The nearest facilities were six miles away and consisted of a mercantile, with a gas pump and rental movies, a small cafe, and a laundromat, with the latter having running water and hot showers.

With minimal social exposure and my not working, the children and I spent many hours together, exploring the woods and trails. At thirteen, Sarah often worked on Chuck's survey crew, consisting of him and one other helper. She had the time of her life and daily came home with new stories of her feats.

When Sarah had a tantrum as a small child, she repeatedly told me she hated me, which hurt me a great deal. Dan never disciplined her for these behaviors, and I believe he secretly enjoyed her treatment of me. He seemed to need all of the children's affection and felt threatened if they showed me love. During the years following the divorce, Dan continually negated me to the children because of his unresolved anger toward me and his mother. During those summer evenings in Alaska, after I had gone to bed, Sarah often came to lay next to me for a few minutes and talk. For those precious moments, I felt my daughter valued and needed me as her mother.

At eleven, Jeffrey was in his element in Alaska. He was an avid fisherman, so he and I frequently wet our hooks in the streams. When the salmon were running, Chuck took us to the river. To prevent Jeffrey from being pulled into the rapid current, we tied a rope around his waist and attached it to a tree. In such a pose, Jeffrey lived every boy's dream. He caught a forty pounder.

When Billy came, we all had fun giving him an Alaskan tour. Billy particularly wanted to catch a salmon, but after much fishing, to his disappointment, he was unable to hook one. Billy's visit was awkward. I so wanted to connect with him, but he held me at arm's length. His anger toward me was palpable and felt subject to erupt at a moment's notice. I feared he would again sever our relationship, so I walked carefully around him, as if I was barefoot on broken glass. However, toward the end of his visit, I felt Billy soften a bit toward me and, on his departure, I was hopeful that I would again see my son.

After the children returned to their respective homes, Chuck and I made divorce arrangements. We said our goodbyes, and the first day of August of 1995, while Chuck was away on a job, I hitched the twenty-three foot 1983 camping trailer to the Suburban, my only possessions, and headed for Oklahoma. My only companion was Sam, who came to me as a puppy from the mercantile porch. Tied to a post, he bore a sign reading, "Take me home," so I did. Sam was black with brown markings, a German shepherd-huskie mix. At seven months, he was hefty and extremely protective. Under Sam's watchful eyes, I felt completely safe. Besides for backup, I carried a small revolver. I might not be able to hit much, but the noise would scare them to death.

As I departed Alaska, I felt my mission there was complete. During my stay, I had helped other trauma survivors, and my own healing had progressed. At times, during my sojourn, my rational mind attempted to disclaim the reality of my trauma but, when this occurred, my subconscious mind, while I was awake and asleep, gave me a movie reel refresher course of each event. While in Alaska, my last vestiges of denial were crushed, and I traversed the final integration of my trauma. As I crossed the Alaskan border into Canada, I looked forward to the revelation of God's plan for my life.

In my brown Suburban with travel trailer in tow, Sam and I traversed the Canadian "highways," which often bore resemblance to rough country roads. After changing many flat tires and adding considerable water to the radiator, we crossed into the Lower 48. I was so glad to be out of Canada, I promptly shredded my Canadian maps and vowed to never travel there again. Anyway, in my estimation, as far as scenery goes, Canada is a poor stepchild to Alaska.

I hadn't been in the continental United States during the summer for five years, and the Suburban had no air-conditioning. As Sam and I drove south, we had a four-sixty cooling system, four windows down at sixty miles an hour. As I drove through the countryside, my senses came alive, and I saw plants, smelled scents, and heard sounds I had long forgotten.

Each evening, we stopped along the side of the road or in parks and ate, exercised, and rested. Sam was my loving protector and companion.

Going around a sharp curve shortly after entering Idaho, the trailer hit a soft gravel shoulder and jack-knifed. In slow motion, I knew I was powerless and possibly doomed. I just prayed and held onto the steering wheel. Coming toward me around the curve was a Volkswagen. The driver immediately turned to the opposing ditch. By God's grace, no one was hurt, and the truck, trailer, and Volkswagen remained undamaged. After all motion ceased, the man driving the Volkswagen hopped out and began swearing and screaming at me. Crying, I got back into the truck, rolled up the windows, and prayed. I couldn't deal with the man's abuse and refused to listen. Shortly, a policeman came who was very courteous. He calmed the man and comforted me, and soon we were all on our way.

After fourteen days and over four thousand miles, Sam and I spent our last night on the road camped in the Texas panhandle. The following morning, we made a ritual of crossing the Oklahoma state line. As we drove through western Oklahoma, the fields were being prepared for the planting of winter wheat. As the sun glistened off the newly-plowed red earth and the scent filled my nostrils, I knew my roots were in Oklahoma, and I was home.

1. Yogananda, 1990, 16-17.

CHAPTER NINE

Reclaiming My Roots

♀

SAM AND I ARRIVED IN OKLAHOMA CITY on August 15, 1995, and set up camp at a park for recreational vehicles. Alaska taught me to keep it simple and freed me from the hostage of "modern conveniences," so I knew I could be comfortable in the trailer for an indefinite period.

I had just enough money to rent and furnish an office and provide my basic needs for about two months. I hit the ground running. By the first of September, I was ready to see patients and had visited local and surrounding rural drug and alcohol treatment centers and psychiatric hospitals. I wanted to explore the lay of the land and to announce I was ready for work.

With a little advertising, my practice developed gradually. To pay the bills, two days a week I saw patients in two rural clinics, each eighty miles from my home base.

Never being one to give up easily on anything, that winter I briefly attempted to reconcile with Chuck. I met him in Las Vegas, where he was working. For us to get back together, he stated I must "share completely." Well, that hit me up by the side of the head. What kind of deal was that? He always shared his bills and my money. I was done.

After my return from Alaska and understandably so, Sarah and Jeffrey didn't want their school, friends, or routines to be disrupted by me, so they continued to reside with their father. At this time, Sarah was a very rebellious and angry teenager, had her father trained, and had no desire for me to interfere with her reign of control in her father's home, so she kept me at bay by her hostility and verbal abuse. Jeffrey was heavily influenced by his sister and father, and Dan continued to malign me to the children on a regular basis. Even so, Jeffrey occasionally spent time with me, and I believe we both enjoyed it immensely.

For several years, I had longed to return to farm life. Sam and I ventured to look at a few farms, but I feared the loneliness and isolation, so the following February, I decided to purchase a new home in Oklahoma City. I planned to propose an offer on Monday, but life and God had other plans.

On the preceding Thursday afternoon, the park manager told me he had complaints about Sam, and I needed to get rid of him. I was going to a rural clinic the next day and, as I prepared for bed that night, I prayed for God to help me find a new home for Sam. I decided since it was Sam's last night at the park, I would let him roam and say good-bye to his buddies. At 2:00 a.m. on Friday morning, a livid park manager pounded on my door. He demanded Sam and I both leave by noon that day. I said it was impossible because I had to be at work in a distant town by 9:00 a.m. The manager commented that fact was not his problem, and I instinctively knew he was the type who would relish impounding my home.

For awhile, I went back to bed and cried. Then I decided I was not going to let that so and so beat me. Only once, in broad daylight, had I hitched the trailer to the truck. At 3:00 a.m., with flashlight in hand, I was securing the hitch and began to laugh. I realized that I had prayed the night before for a new home for Sam, little knowing I was going to get one too. By 7:00 a.m., Sam, my trailer, truck, and I were on the road to my rural clinic.

After work that day, I was exhausted and didn't know where to go. I was torn between wanting to keep Sam and knowing he could be a nuisance, and we would probably be evicted from another trailer park before I could close on the house. That evening, I cried, prayed, and went to bed. I awoke bolt-upright at 2:00 a.m. on Saturday and knew exactly where I needed to go. I had a friend, John, with a sixteen-acre farm thirty miles outside of Oklahoma City, where he had offered to allow me to park the trailer, but I had been afraid of the loneliness.

By 10:00 a. m., my truck, trailer, Sam, and I were on the road, but we had a new companion, a stray black Labrador puppy, Ben, who had followed us home from our morning walk.

Immediately upon setting up camp on the farm, I knew this was where I was supposed to be. I drank in the sun, earth, and my privacy. Loneliness was a non-issue. I felt surrounded by God and nature. I knew that God, through Sam and the park manager, had grabbed me by the seat of the pants before I sold myself short by buying a house in town, and the park manager and Sam had given me the jump-start I needed to take the leap toward my heart's desire.

On the farm, the trailer was parked near an old cattle pen which was overgrown with weeds. I decided the pen would make an ideal garden spot, so that spring, with shovel in hand, I turned over the soil and cleared it of weeds. With manure from animals long gone and with vigilant weeding and watering, my garden prospered. I grew lush yellow squash, vines heavy laden with green beans, and okra plants that towered over my head. I enjoyed sharing my harvest with my friends and neighbors and, with the labor, sun, and fresh air, my body gained strength, luxuriated in its power, and yearned for more.

That spring, I learned the owner of the contiguous 144 acres wanted to sell, and we struck a deal. The land consisted of rolling hills, a valley, and an overgrowth of brush and trees. I walked the land, found its highest point located near its eastern border, and planned to build my home there facing west, the valley, and the rise of the next hill.

To access my proposed home site, I built a driveway over a ditch. I could have hired someone to do it, but part of the adventure was doing it myself at minimal cost. I placed the driveway at the top of the hill, so it would drain to the north and south. Canvassing for the throwaways of others, I filled the ditch with old tires and irregular rocks, brick, and pieces of concrete and covered them with dirt. Later in the summer, with a few glasses of lemonade, I befriended the African-American highway crew, who were patching the blacktop on my section line. For my kindness, they deposited their leftover asphalt mix on my driveway. I felt very blessed.

To maximize my time on the farm, I created an office schedule in which I saw patients three to four days a week and worked on the farm the remaining days. My building site was occupied by wall-to-wall brush. With a chain saw and tree trimmers, I methodically and laboriously cleared an ever widening circle, which after six years consists of five acres. I stuffed my Suburban with the brush and deposited it down the hill in an erosion gully beneath one of the three ponds and delighted in my self-sufficiency.

Before moving the trailer to the hill, I hired crews to dig the septic system and drill a well. Those two chores were beyond the scope of my shovel. On John's sixteen acres, I didn't have a septic system, so the trailer sewage could only expel "gray water," meaning I had to be creative in disposal of excrement, so I lined the stool with a plastic bag, did my business, then double bagged it in my trash, which I disposed of in my office's dumpster. On Billy's first visit to the farm, he couldn't quite get over his mother, "The Doctor," shitting, to use his word, in a plastic bag. Myself, I considered it a creative solution.

During the same visit, I wanted to show Billy the farm. For the trek, I wore long pants and boots and cautioned Billy to do the same. He felt that was unnecessary and wore sandals and shorts. Little did he know how large the farm was or the extent of his mother's physical stamina. By the time we approached the building site, he was ready to walk on asphalt, so we took the long way back to the trailer. I didn't dare laugh out loud, but I internally chuckled. My son from the city presumed he, with his male prowess, would lay his mother in the shade. I wasn't the one with aching feet that night.

After setting up the trailer on my house site, my only electrical source was a generator. I discovered the gatekeeper to the building codes was the electric company. I resolutely refused to give anyone permission to dictate how I built my home in the middle of 144 acres, so I streamlined my electrical needs to a water pump, lights, and television. My air-conditioning was an open window and a breeze, and my refrigerator, range, and heat were powered by propane. After reading about various sources of electrical energy, I decided my new home would be powered by a combination of generators, solar panels, and eventually fuel cells.

Once while visiting Eagle, Alaska, I saw a seventy-six-year-old woman splitting logs with an axe. She was my role model. I figured if I built my own home, as a little old lady, I could repair it. I read about underground, rammed earth, cobb, and hay-bale houses. After much deliberation and before winter set in, I proceeded to build a prototype hay-bale structure to house my water pump and generator. My main building consultants were books, pamphlets, and the owner of the local lumberyard, Richard. I would go into the small nearby town of Luther, consult Richard on my ideas, then have him deliver the materials. Digging holes two feet wide and three feet deep, I set fourteen-foot, four-by-four treated posts in concrete. When I placed my first post, I proudly stepped back to survey my handiwork. I knew if I could set one post, I could set a hundred and therefore build my own home. For all of my building projects to come, I worked on a square grid system, with posts every four to eight to sixteen feet.

When I began on the generator-well house, I was forty-nine and had never used a hammer for anything more than hanging a picture, but I discovered I had a pretty mean swing. After the posts were in place, I joined them with two-by-sixes, placed rafters, and made a slanted roof of corrugated metal.

My Uncle Fred was a master carpenter, and I watched him rebuild my childhood home after the fire. With many parts of fingers missing, Uncle Fred carefully measured, cut, and nailed each board. His blood runs in my veins, and what I lacked in skill I made up for in heart and creativity. As I pounded nails and fashioned my first roof, I decided carpentry was a lot like making a dress, and I had made dresses since I was twelve.

After completing the roof, I built a concrete perimeter foundation. I paid the children a generous wage, and Jeffrey helped me muscle the hay bales into place and secure them with rebar and wire. The walls, to say the least, were a little irregular. I was delighted when Sarah helped me cover the interior and exterior walls with swirls of red-earth plaster. There is a deep communion that occurs between two people working together, and Sarah and I became closer as we worked. About the plastering, Sarah said, "It's like making a giant sculpture." For me, the walls were perfectly beautiful in their irregularities. My children and I had completed our first building project.

On the morning of December 16, 1996, I held a groundbreaking ceremony for my home. It was the day of my fiftieth birthday. Those in attendance were my dogs, the birds, and myself. It was a glorious morning and enjoyed by all celebrants.

One Saturday morning the following January, both generators were down, therefore my propane heating system was defunct without its electrical fan. The temperature read seventeen degrees Fahrenheit, and bed was the warmest place to be. As I sat huddled under the covers hand-stitching quilting blocks, I was suddenly seized with the need to write an article.

For years, friends asked when I planned to write a book. I would smile and say, "When it's time." In writing academic papers, all the life and joy is absent after the prodding and kneading of the scientific method, but this was something new. The words flowed from a source deep within. It was as if the cosmic computer had pressed print, and thoughts spilled onto paper. Within a few months, I had written over three hundred short essays, which later developed into *Red Earth Wisdom*.

After the birth of my writer self, I realized once again God's hand was present. Without electricity, the world's chatter was silenced, and I could hear my inner voice. My writing had been gestating within me, and its time had come.

BILLY

With mending, my relationship with Billy exceeded my greatest hopes. Billy invited me to visit, and one or two times a year I flew north and explored our nation's capitol, with my son as my guide. At various times, my visits included taking in a George Washington University or, at that time, a Washington Bullets basketball game or a Baltimore Ravens football game. Billy rarely exhibited hostility toward me. Together, we laughed, talked, and grew close.

As I was departing after one such visit, Billy told me he was "sad" and said, "Mom, I will miss you." My heart was full.

Midway through law school, Billy's spirits were low and his goal seemed overwhelming. To rouse his flagging spirits, I proposed his graduation present, a two-week trip to Europe for the two of us. Billy was to plan the itinerary, with the only exception being a few days in Florence, a must for me.

In flying colors and as editor of the law review, Billy graduated in May of 1997. The day of conferring Billy's degree in jurisprudence was honored by his walking, in his cap and gown, the many blocks from his home to the site of the graduation ceremony. On this walk, as I accompanied him and his girlfriend of five years, Sandy, they off-handedly spoke of marriage and my future grandchildren. For Billy, his graduation appeared to mark his passage into manhood and his future roles of husband and father.

In August, Billy and I left for Italy. We were accompanied by his friend Chris and Chris' mother, Mary. The three of them planned and organized the trip, and I just enjoyed the fruits of their labor.

Much to my delight, we were to spend the entire two weeks in Italy, with the boys going on to Switzerland for a third week. The trip glows in the annals of my memory as a blessed time with my son.

My friend David once said, "It's a good life if you don't weaken," which speaks to me of persistence, patience, and endurance. My traveling companions and I arrived in Venice after traveling over twenty-four hours by car, plane, bus, train, boat, and foot, in that order. On arriving, I definitely was weakening, but I did persist and endure, even though, at times, I was a little short on patience.

After resting, we began our exploration of Venice. We stayed near the Piazza San Marco, with its vendors, pigeons, and string quartets. Venice's narrow, winding streets were filled with people, pets, and couples, and the renowned Venetian waterways were navigated by many gondolas and motor boats. Venice's shop windows were filled with multicolored glass, lace, and masks of all descriptions.

The four of us toured the Basilica San Marco with its glittering, golden ceilings and art of many dates and styles. In the Ducal Palace, we viewed the wood and picture-lined council chambers and its prison.

What I will remember most about Venice is its sense of art, passion, and sensuality. Venice truly is a city for lovers.

From Venice, we traveled to Florence. For eleven years, I anticipated my return to Florence and its Botticellis, Raphaels, Titians, Michelangelos, palaces, and cathedrals. As I meandered her streets and revisited the sites of my previous tour, I was not disappointed. From Florence, we drove through the country, stopping in Pisa and on to La Spezia and Monterosso. On our drive, we viewed mountain-top villas surrounded by tall willowy trees, fields of sunflowers and olive trees, and hillsides covered with vineyards. We saw villages perched atop mountains and nestled on hillsides and mountain faces cut away by the quarrying of marble, with roadside marble storage yards filled with slabs of polished stone, and everywhere was the loud, screeching, renowned Italian bumper-car traffic.

When we reached the Mediterranean, I began my love affair with the sea. On the beach at Monterosso were rows of umbrellas and an abundance of sunbathers of all sizes and descriptions. There were frolicking, sometimes nude, children, bronzed perfect bodies of adolescence and young adulthood, and, best of all, older bodies each beautiful and perfect in their uniqueness.

I didn't own a swim suit. On viewing European women in every size, age, shape, description, and nationality wearing single and two-piece bathing suits, with an occasional topless bather, I promptly marched to a nearby shop and bought a two-piece and joined them. These women did not hide their bodies. They were there to bathe and luxuriate in the sea, and they did so with gusto. These women were my teachers, and I delighted in their lessons.

Continuing our experience of the Italian Riviera, we traveled to Santa Margherita Ligure and my favorite hotel owned by a delightful English lady, Mrs. Fasce, and her Italian husband. The hotel was built in levels on a hillside, as was the town. With the sea beckoning below, our rooms opened to a flower-laden terrace, where mornings I could be found writing.

Through our trip and sightseeing, Billy and I had a nice ebb and flow. At times we explored together. Other times, we each needed solitude, or Billy needed time with Chris, so we went our separate ways. When alone, I walked through the town and bought water, fruit, and bread, then descended to the beach, with its smooth stones of all sizes and colors, forged in the giant tumbler of the sea. I sat on the beach or laid on huge boulders as the azure water lapped around and mesmerized me with its soothing melodic rhythms.

Another delight of the trip was observing Europeans on holiday, with their pets and bambinos. In my study, I saw a rare leashed or caged cat and a wide array of dogs. There was a Doberman Pinscher that intimidated a spaniel puppy. There were frequent German shepherds, collies, bulldogs, dachshunds, and poodles and a number of terrier varieties, especially Scottish terriers. There were spaniels of all breeds and colors and even one black-and-white spotted creature, a cross with a

poodle. Then there were the many varieties of miniature, wad-
dling, fur balls, and of course, there were those dogs only God
knew the lineage.

Then came the bambinos, from newborns to toddlers pushed
in all description of carriages. There were smiling cherubs with
two front teeth, bambinos with no hair to thick curly black,
brown, blonde, or red hair, and daring toddlers chasing pigeons
or cars, who were hastily retrieved by parents or grandparents.

From the sea, we traveled north to the lake country. During
our last days together, Billy and I took the car and explored
small villages with narrow winding streets, which scarcely allowed room for one vehicle to pass. We laughed uproariously
and shared our most intimate moments of the trip. Billy asked
about his childhood and some of the decisions I made. I cried
and shared but couldn't begin to convey to my son the journey I
had traversed, because Billy didn't want to know the truth about
his grandparents, and I respected his desire to protect his relationship with them.

My trauma compounded with the social revolution of the
sixties was difficult to explain to a young man in his twenties.
The sixties were a time of wholesale revolution against all existing standards and norms. There were protests against the
war in Vietnam, with sit-ins, stand-ins, demonstrations, and
take-overs. There were protests against the lack of women's
rights exemplified by bra-burning and the changing order of the
home. There were protests against previous moral standards,
with "free love and sex" and, of course, there was the flowering
of the drug culture. In the sixties, the family system was tested,
shaken, and nearly destroyed, and individuals of my generation

were confused. The world as we had known it was in chaos, and this was the environment in which my son was born. Out of my confusion, my son experienced many wounds, which I deeply regret but, in spite of my lack of mothering skills, he had grown into a resilient, learned man, with wisdom beyond his years. As we talked, my son emitted a silent peace, understanding, and forgiveness for our relationship's journey and pain and, on a deep level, I felt reconciled with and loved by my son. That moment was worth all the pain I endured with his absence.

As Mary and I prepared for our departure from Malpensa to Chicago and on to Oklahoma, with the boys seeing us off before traveling on to Switzerland, I reflected how Billy's law school graduation present was a gift to me of time with my son before he entered the next phase of his life, which would include his law practice and probable marriage and birth of my grandchildren.

VICTORIA'S CORSET

After my return from Italy, it was the middle of August, and I was scheduled to see patients the next day. I was excited to be home and ready to get some exercise and do a little work on the house. By this time, Jeffrey, Sarah, and I had dug and set forty-two posts in concrete, and I had joined the posts with two-by-sixes and was working on the high cross-beams on which the rafters would rest. With the heat and my fatigue, I became careless and stepped out onto air. In the moments it took for me to fall twelve feet, I prayed for God's will and care. As my bottom hit the ground, I felt my spinal column buckle like an accordion. Instantly, I knew I would be lucky to walk again. As I lay on the ground wracked in pain, I continued to pray. Eventually, I collected myself and realized all of my limbs were moving. With "utter brilliance," I managed to get to my feet, compulsively put away my tools, and go in the trailer.

My friend, David, took me to the emergency room. I was in excruciating pain as I was moved for each X-ray, but I refused medications. I wanted to be clear-minded to make decisions if surgery was indicated. I had a fractured sternum and T-10 vertebrae, but my spinal cord wasn't involved. For financial reasons, I refused to stay in the hospital, because I have no truck with insurance companies and consider them a legalized form of theft.

David took me home by way of the office. Since I was and am a one woman office, I had to collect phone numbers for my patients scheduled for the following day. The next morning, after many phone calls, I went into town and visited an orthopedist, who sent me to be fitted for a Jewett-brace, a metal contraption that enclosed me from collar-bone to pelvis, which I laughingly called my "Victoria's Secret corset." The following day, I saw patients. I figured I could hurt at home or the office, and I might as well do something useful.

My house building was put on a lengthy hold. As my back mended and my strength returned, I tackled smaller projects that were low to the ground. I find physical labor exhilarating, and it works out all kinds of kinks and tension in my body and mind. Exercise may not grant eternal youth, but it sure makes growing older a lot more fun. With David's help and me still in my brace, I decided to add a west porch onto the trailer, which developed into a full-scale wood-frame "doublewide," as Billy called it. Later, free of my brace but wearing back support, I braved my fear and roofed the new one-room addition. Because

I was hungry for color, pattern, and beauty, David helped me wallpaper the new walls. He also helped me install a wood stove for my heat source, and I already had a winter's stack of firewood from my yard clearing and tree pruning.

Following completion of the new room, through summers and winters, alone I proceeded to add an east porch extending the length of the trailer. Then, I added a carport, which connected the trailer to the sixteen-by-sixteen-foot generator/well house located to the north. On the same grid pattern, I built a sixteen-by-forty-eight-foot barn as an extension to the north side of the generator/well house. As I dug each posthole, I continued to be amazed by the Oklahoma soil, which consists of thick layers of red clay interspersed with dark loam. As I handled the thick rich clumps of clay, I knew this was the substance from which the Indians had shaped their pots. Digging hole after hole, I felt a deep kinship with the red earth, and my roots sank far deeper than those of the posts.

I sided the barn with plywood, since the hay bales were too labor intensive, and the barn was for storage of tools and equipment and didn't require the thermal factors that the hay bales provided. As I traversed up and down the ladder putting in place the various corrugated metal roofs, I gained expertise and confidence to again tackle the height of the house.

HATCHING

In the winter of 1998, in the middle of my various building projects, Jeffrey, at fourteen, was incubating a dozen chicken eggs in his bedroom, which were given to him by my friend and neighbor, Jean Anne. Two weeks later out hatched Fred and

Mollie. While waiting for the expected hatchings, to the north of the barn which was still under construction, Jeffrey and I built a chicken house inside a pen, originally built for a goat named "Uni," who reminded me of a unicorn. Uni was such a pain in the back-side that when he ran away I decided to let nature take its course and didn't go look for him, not that I could have found him anyway.

While Fred and Mollie were residing in my living room in the process of growing and going from fuzz to feathers, we discovered we had waited too long for our new addition Caroline's visit to the veterinarian. Gorgeous George, a beautiful Huskie, had come to court, and we were expecting. Before Fred and Mollie could take up residence in their new home, Caroline gave birth, in the chicken house, to a brood of nine. After Caroline had weaned her pups and I found new homes for them, Fred and Mollie were able to set up housekeeping.

The following spring, I purchased new members for the poultry yard, but that summer my flock dwindled as they flew out, becoming dog food, and the hawks and owls flew into the pen for dinner. I lost Mollie that summer, but Fred grew into a powerful strutting cock, with tail and wing feathers of black and emerald laced with gold. Fred was later displaced by his sparring partner, Pete.

To halt the attrition of my fowl population, I decided to build an aviary, also known as putting a lid on my chicken pen. The aviary's wood rafters were painted dark brown and supported chicken-wire. Under the roof were perches, the chicken yard, and chicken house, with the latter painted beige and brown to match the barn and trailer additions. I later circled the exterior of the pen with flowerbeds and planted rosebushes. After completing my aviary, I stepped back, surveyed my handiwork, and concluded it surely had to be the fanciest chicken pen in the county.

In the meantime, I was seeing patients thirty hours a week and writing profusely, the latter including the initial drafts of this book and my third book, *Renaissance Woman*.

During this period, because I dreaded the laundromat, I washed my clothes by hand in the bathtub and hung them on the clothesline and, for ironing, I heated two antique flatirons by the flame of my gas range. I enjoyed these simple tasks and felt connected with the women of times past.

ANOTHER BOMBING

On the evening of May 3, 1999, thirty-six tornadoes roared through Oklahoma, some with F-4 to F-6 magnitudes. By television, I, along with many other Oklahomans, watched and listened in horror as meteorologists followed the deadly storms. As the evening unfolded, a wedge-shaped one-half to three-fourths mile-wide tornado tracked through southern Oklahoma City. We viewers were told that our best chance of survival would be in underground shelters. On the farm, I had no such shelter. Those without shelters were instructed to go to the center of their homes in a bathroom or closet and cover and surround themselves with pillows and blankets. I was not overly concerned because the storm was moving south and east of my home, but suddenly the meteorologist reported the storm had turned north, and I knew the farm was in its direct path. I looked out my front door and saw the wide black funnel headed toward me. I prayed, gathered blankets and pillows, and headed to the bathroom. I knew that a trailer is dangerous to occupy during a tornado and realized this might be my time to die. I prayed for God's will to prevail. I heard a sound resembling a train then deadly silence. I felt suction and knew the tornado was directly overhead. As I continued to pray, I began to feel a sweet peace come over me. I knew to the core of my being that God surrounded me and that I was safe. Shortly, the stormed passed. My heart was filled with gratitude. I looked about me in the bathroom and saw dust-bunnies residing on the ceiling that had formerly occupied the floor. The next morning, I went out to assess the damage and was amazed to see almost everything intact. All of my laboriously constructed buildings were unharmed. The periphery of the yard had an eighteen-inch in diameter tree that had snapped and been drug several feet. I felt deeply blessed.

On that May night, forty-one people were killed from ages three weeks to eighty-six years, and more than six hundred people were injured. Twelve thousand cars and three-hundred-and-fifty homes were destroyed. The people of Oklahoma City were in shock. The storm felt like the Murrah Building bombing all over again. As always, Oklahomans roused themselves and banded together. City organizations collected food, water, and supplies for the victims. Children donated their toys and allowances. Anonymous acts of kindness began to occur. People donated flower seed, water sprinklers, furniture, baby supplies, clothes, money, and themselves. Survivors made us laugh with painted signs on the wreckage of their homes reading, "Hey Dorothy" and "A real fixer-upper." The governor heralded our resilient spirit, and I felt prouder than ever to be an Oklahoman.

My First Grandchild

In late May of 1999, as Sarah prepared to graduate from high school, she informed me with trepidation that she was pregnant. I calmly took in the information and asked her what she wanted to do. I told her I would love a grandchild, but the pregnancy was her decision, and I supported her choice either way. Sarah cried in relief, stating she wanted her child. With joy and anticipation, we talked of the baby. Her father had told Sarah that I would become hysterical on hearing the news, which was the ultimate in projecting his feelings onto me. Because Sarah refused an abortion and was adopted into her boyfriend Carlos' Catholic Hispanic family and home, Dan distanced himself from her during the pregnancy.

During this time, without Dan's triangulation for Sarah's affection, Sarah and I experienced a closeness we had not known since our last summer together in Alaska. I embraced Carlos' family and found his parents, seven siblings, their spouses, and children to be the epitome of a loving, supportive family system in which the rearing of children is their primary concern.

On November 26th of that year, Sarah gave birth to my grandson, Carlos. Being a family event, Dan, Carlos, two of Carlos' sisters, and I were in the birthing suite. I was privileged to observe and deeply touched as Carlos Senior lovingly tended Sarah through her labor. I felt profoundly blessed as I viewed the birth of my grandson. I was soon to discover Sarah to be an excellent mother.

House Building

For three years the skeleton of my house had projected into the air, and it was screaming for completion so, in February of

2000, I resumed construction. The house stood to the south of the trailer complex and faced west. The house was thirty-two by forty feet, with additional eight-foot-wide porches extending its length on the west and east sides.

For safety, I first built a wood plank platform, which was to be the internal ceiling, and for additional support, I overlaid the planks with plywood. Then, from the platform, I completed the cross beams and set the rafters.

Building was interrupted that May when Jeffrey and I traveled to Washington, D.C., and attended Billy and Sandy's wedding. Sandy, Billy, and Sandy's mother had meticulously planned the wedding and adhered to tradition. Because of the trauma of my multiple spouses, Billy was gun-shy of marriage and had wisely waited until he knew he could make a lifetime commitment, which was reflected in the marriage ceremony. After the ceremony, I was touched deeply when Billy asked me to read the "Apache Wedding Prayer" as a toast to them, the newly wedded couple. Later, Sandy, an elegant and beautiful bride on her father's arm, led the dancing. Shortly thereafter, to my surprise, Billy escorted me onto the dance floor. As my son held me in his arms and honored me as his mother, tears streamed down my face.

After the wedding, I returned home and decided the house wasn't big enough so, with Jeffrey's help and by adding more four-by-four posts, I extended the south wall an additional twelve feet, making the north-south length of the house fifty-two feet.

After completing the framing of the extension, I began roofing. Of course, I wouldn't want to do anything the easy way, so I roofed my house in July. As in my other buildings, I used corrugated metal and covered each roofing nail with silicon caulk. I didn't plan for water to dribble on my head.

While on the roof one day, I heard a gunshot and saw Sam run up to the trailer. I had a neighbor who I suspected had shot many of my adopted strays, so I watched Sam for awhile as he lay near the trailer. He looked fine, so I didn't go down to investigate. The next morning, Sam was nowhere to be found. I looked under the trailer and saw his lifeless form. With a heavy heart, I dug a grave at the edge of the yard and reverently covered my faithful companion's body. With tears streaming, I prayed over Sam and set a large chunk of red sandstone as a headstone, and to this day, I feel Sam's spirit hover about me.

As roofing continued on the front porch, I took a fall from a ladder and, with a good bounce, fractured a rib in two sites. After a broken back, I wasn't going to let a small thing like a rib slow me down.

Again with shovel in hand and occasionally with Jeffrey's grumbling help, I dug the trench for the stem wall, and David helped us set the stem wall forms. Then, I placed a grid of steel rebar in the trench. When the man delivering the concrete saw my steel work and the width and depth of my trench, he said, "You have enough support to build a two-story rock house." His comment pleased me. I never wanted to be shy on materials. The stem wall surrounded the previously set four-by-four posts of the exterior wall, which encased the posts in a total depth of five feet of concrete. There were no puny studs bolted to a concrete slab for my house. As in my concrete work and throughout the construction of the house, if an extra board, nail, or brace might be indicated, I put it there. I wanted the house to see me through my "golden years" and withstand Oklahoma's high winds and tornadoes.

With a little help from David, Carlos Sr., and his broth-ers, Jeffrey and I dug out the grass and dirt within the stem wall. Now mind you, I wasn't using slave labor. Each time the children worked for me, I paid them an ample hourly wage. Unfortunately, to say the least, Jeffrey didn't have my passion for the project. David laid the plumbing system by my design speci-fications because, of course, I was the architect. With Jeffrey and David's help and one shovel full at a time, we filled the space within the stem wall with several loads of sand.

Again our friend delivered concrete, and we poured the slab in three sections because that was all, on any one day, Jeffrey, David, and I could handle.

More often than not, I worked alone until dusk. After many of those long hot summer work days, I had a refreshing nude dip in my country version of a swimming pool, a horse trough, with-out the horse. When one lives alone behind a locked steel gate in the middle of 144 acres, there are delightful liberties one can take. With the stars and moon overhead, it doesn't get much bet-ter than cooling off in a clean pool of water, for my horse trough was scrubbed and filled with fresh water on a regular basis.

By now, the house was taking form, and I was excited. Having occupied the trailer for five years, even with the room addition, I was long overdue for a "real" house. Between each four-by-four post, I began framing, with a vengeance, the studs, windows, and doors. I was like a horse with the scent of the barn door and grain in its nostrils. I was on a dead run to have the house enclosed for Thanksgiving dinner.

After framing, I installed the windows. For the view and max-imum summer airflow and minimum winter heat loss, I placed a row of windows on the west and south, a few on the east, and none on the north. My air-conditioning was to be the summer breezes, and my central heat was a potbellied stove in the middle of the house, with a propane backup when necessary.

The exterior insulation board went up next. After observing the deterioration of the hay bales and plaster of the generator/ well house, I determined the upkeep of that building method was too labor intensive, so I decided to use cedar and rock for my home's exterior. Staying true to my roots, I selected gray Oklahoma limestone, which was delivered and dumped in two large piles. David showed me how to get started, and I was off. I loved the colors and shapes of the rocks and how they went together like a puzzle. The largest ones were on the bottom three rows, and some stones were so heavy I couldn't pick them up and had to roll them up an incline. On the north side, the entire wall was rock. On the remaining sides of the house, I rocked to the lower window ledges and used treated cedar planks around and above the windows. Slowly and methodically, I circled the house, laying one to two rows of stones at a time.

Once, while cementing a new row of rocks about four feet off the ground, I became careless, and as I bent over to pick up another rock, three large stones slid from the wall and hit me in the back of the head. I lay on the ground and cried for awhile. I then assessed my condition. My thinking and vision were clear, and my motor skills weren't impaired. I surmised the only thing I could possibly develop was an intracerebral hemorrhage, which may or may not have advance-warning signs. After I broke my back, I didn't relish another emergency room visit, so I decided it was either my time to die or it wasn't, and only God could determine that, so with a prayer for God's will to be done, I got up from the ground and laid some more rock.

The work continued all summer and fall. My days away from the office were devoted to the house and were eight to twelve hours long. By the week before Thanksgiving, all of the walls were enclosed. Thanksgiving week, I had wood doors delivered and hung and a propane heater installed. Though the interior was unfinished, we had a roof, walls, windows, doors, and heat. As with all my electrical needs, I ran a cord from the generator located in the generator/well house and used droplights. As far as I was concerned, the house was ready for its first Thanksgiving.

Billy and Sandy arrived on Wednesday before Thanksgiving and were suitably impressed with my building endeavors. On Thanksgiving Day, I covered my worktable, also known as a picnic table, with a festive tablecloth and set it with candles and my collection of antique Bavarian china. In honor of the occasion, a friend sent me a beautiful floral arrangement for a centerpiece. In the trailer and with Billy's help, I prepared a turkey with all the trimmings. Jeffrey, Sarah, Carlos, and little Carlos, who was by then walking, helped Billy, Sandy, and me ferry the dinner to the new house. With the knowledge of the sacredness of the occasion, in warmth, merriment, and a true spirit of thanksgiving, we ate our meal, as little Carlos blissfully circled the table. Surrounded by my children and grandchild, I felt deeply blessed, and my heart brimmed with love and gratitude.

♀ ♀ ♀

As the light dims with the setting sun, I awake from my reverie, gather my quilting materials and a day's worth of newly stitched quilt blocks, and enter the house.

CHAPTER TEN

The Adventure Continues

♀

My years on the farm were peaceful and, in my solitude, I walked close to the earth and God. Living essentially in
seclusion, I built my home and was aware that I was attempting
to recreate an environment similar to my Grandmother Ollie's
Arkansas home and its feeling of warmth and safety. Even
though at times I felt lonely and isolated, I tenaciously held
to the idea that I would live the remainder of my years on the
farm.

I eventually realized the time for the farm and its lessons had
passed. I no longer needed to reject the world and lock myself
behind closed gates on a large acreage to feel safe and peaceful. I
sold the farm.

I now live in Oklahoma City. My home is peaceful and sur-
rounds me in loving energy. My home is not a replica of my
grandmother's, but her presence is ever with me. My home is an
eclectic reflection of me, but my security and self-worth are in
no way attached to my home or its contents. Its exterior is surrounded by flowerbeds and, at planting time, I dig into the earth
and find layers of rich red Oklahoma clay.

I live in solitude, comfort, and happiness. I want for nothing, because God abundantly provides. I spend many hours in silence doing the sacred, the ordinary, in life. The remainder of my hours are filled with my patients, writing, children, grandchildren, and friends.

I love the rhythm and flow of my life, which is in congruence with my soul. I am peaceful and serene at my center and grateful for all my life's lessons, including my childhood trauma, because it forged the being I have become. With God's bellows, my trauma tempered my spirit to a resilient state, without which I would be a far weaker and less compassionate person.

In the context of my childhood trauma, I understand the roots of my eating disorder and, with the help of Geneen Roth and others, food and weight are non-issues in my life. I have not binged since I first read Roth's work.

I daily ask God to "relieve me of the bondage of self," which includes negative thoughts, feelings, or behaviors toward myself or others. My transformation required being willing to change all of me, every thought, value, and action. To walk in God's light, no part of my being remained untouched.

There have been many times on my healing journey that I knew I must make a change or perish. I felt as if I was backed to the edge of a cliff on a black, stormy night, and my only salvation was to jump and trust God would catch me. Many times, I jumped and always found myself, with God's loving hands, placed on new and fertile soil.

To avoid change, I was often dragged kicking and screaming to those late night rendezvous. Once there, I felt if I did not jump, I would be hurled from the precipice. Again and again, I jumped, and always, God kept me safe from harm. Slowly, I developed a deep, abiding faith and trust in God's care.

No matter its severity, I adamantly believe that anyone can heal from their trauma, but the path is not easy. Healing requires willingness to surrender every aspect of one's life to God.

For my parents, though I continue to remove myself from their toxic environment, I have compassion and forgiveness and feel sad for them in their choices to leave this lifetime with such heavy hearts.

In my marriages, one might think I failed, but I believe each was a teacher on my soul's journey. The first two were based in the intellect and devoid of feelings, a reflection of that phase of my life in which my intellect was my only tool and, because of my untreated trauma, I felt I deserved my husbands' negation. Souls wither in such a space. My last two marriages, on a subconscious level, were reflections of my father, but there were positives. Each of the men affirmed my personhood and, with them, I felt my full range of feelings. Without Bill, I might not have gone to trauma treatment. Chuck helped me experience the depth and breadth of Alaska. I once commented to a friend that I felt embarrassed by my number of marriages, but he responded, "Their number just means that you grew a lot."

I now realize that my four marriages were basically about my search to belong to and be loved by someone and my desire for security and permanence. I now know that security and the only permanence any lifetime can have is belonging to and being loved by oneself and God.

Over the years, as I trusted my intuition to guide me, I made decisions which my ego-self believed would bring logical, socially acceptable conclusions, such as, "Stay married and live happily ever after." Each intuitive decision moved my soul toward its highest good. It is the presumption of my ego to think it knows where the Spirit leads. There were no failures in my marriages, only a mistaken illusion of their purpose.

Healing is an ongoing process with my children, but miracles have occurred as witnessed by one December day after Carlos' second birthday. That morning, I decided to bake Sandy's family Christmas recipes of gingerbread and sugar cookies. With dough chilling in the refrigerator and red, green, yellow, and white icings ready for spreading, Sarah and Carlos arrived unexpectedly. In jovial comradery, the three of us formed a cookie assembly line. I baked and kept Sarah supplied with icing. After the cookies cooled, Sarah cleverly applied icing and sprinkles, while Carlos rearranged and consumed his share of all ingredients. I treasured those harmonious moments with my daughter and reflected on the priceless benefits of aging and grandmotherhood.

After her adolescent warfare and her justified anger toward me and my deficiencies as a mother, Sarah and I have forged a deeper bond. Now twenty-five, Sarah is a wonderful human being and mother to six-year-old Carlos, two-year-old Leticia, and seven-month-old Azriela. Our family has been blessed by Luz, Sarah's husband and the father of Leticia and Azriela. My daughter and I now live in the same neighborhood and, in these rich fall and winter years of my life, I plan to be a more loving and consistent presence in my children and grandchildren's lives.

I am deeply blessed in my relationships with Billy, now thirty-seven, his wife Sandy, my granddaughter Jessica, age four, and my grandson Joey, age one. After Joey's birth, I visited Billy and his family in Washington, D.C. While Sandy stayed home to tend the newborn, Billy and Jessica took me to a basketball game of the now Washington Wizards. As we cheered and laughed, Billy said to me, "Mom, you're an inspiration to me." I was so stunned I nearly fell off my chair. I couldn't believe my ears. After a pause, I asked Billy, "Did I hear you say that I am an inspiration to you?" He replied, "Yes." I then asked, "What do you mean by that?" I heard him reply, "You have accomplished a lot, and your life has been an adventure. You haven't been afraid to walk off the beaten path." I marveled at my son's growth.

With God's protection and love, Jeffrey, at twenty-three, is confused and searching to find his way. As life does for us all, its lessons will shape his character and guide his path.

Over the last few years, I have studied and reflected on the writings of many enlightened teachers whose messages resonate with the marrow of my soul. Particularly of note among these are the works of Yogananda, Eckhart Tolle, and David Hawkins. Hawkins states that life is an "intertwined holographic dance," which eloquently describes my observation that God moves in circles and curves, and I think in straight lines. My finite mind could not conceive of the journey necessary to bring me to my life's fruition. However, God unwaveringly charted my journey as I sought through prayer and meditation to align my consciousness with God's.

I now know our life's journey is a spiritual one and that we incarnate on this planet to be of service to God and man and to learn lessons for our spiritual evolution.

At times, I grow weary of my assigned tasks and lessons and desire to return to the Source, but my work in this lifetime is far from over. So when weariness creeps in, I must pray for God's strength and guidance to do what is before me each day.

Completing this book was such a task. To restore my flagging energy, I retreated to the powerful red earth of the Navajo reservation. For nine days now, I have sojourned on the rim of Tsegi Canyon and drunk in the beauty of this raw land. For a break from my writing, one day I traveled to Antelope Canyon and descended into the earth's crevice carved by the rushing waters finding their way to Lake Powell. Sandwiched between the canyon's corrugated red sandstone walls, I felt as if I was in the vagina of Mother Earth. I was comforted and filled by Her beauty. Other days, I was inspired by the magnificence of Monument Valley, Valley of the Gods, and the Navajo National Monument. The reservation's red soil and jagged pinnacles of red sandstone emit a frequency with which I resonate to the core, and my energy soars.

With my energy restored and my task complete, I must now return to Oklahoma, my roots, and the adventure of my next evolution.

SUGGESTED READINGS

Bee, B. *The Cob Builders Handbook*. Groundworks, Murphy, Oregon, 1997.

Bowlby, L. *Red Earth Wisdom*. Red Earth Publishing, Inc., Oklahoma City, Oklahoma, 2006.

Bowlby, L. *Renaissance Woman*. Red Earth Publishing, Inc., Oklahoma City, Oklahoma, 2006.

Chernin, K. *The Obsession, Reflections on the Tyranny of Slenderness*. First Harper Colophon, New York, New York, 1981.

Cousins, N. *Anatomy of an Illness*. Bantam Books, New York, New York, 1979.

Hawkins, D. *Power Vs. Force*. HayHouse, Inc., Carlsbad, California, 2002.

Hawkins, D. *The Eye of the I*. Veritas, West Sedona, Arizona, 2001.

Hawkins, D. *I*. Veritas, West Sedona, Arizona, 2003.

Hay, L. *The Power Is Within You*. Hay House, Carson, California, 1991.

Hay, L. *You Can Heal Your Life*. Hay House, Santa Monica, California, 1984.

Jampolsky, G. *Teach Only Love*. Bantam Books, New York, New York, 1970.

Jampolsky, G. *Love Is Letting Go of Fear*. Bantam Books, New York, New York, 1979.

Lipton, B. *The Biology of Belief*. Spirit 2000, Inc., Video Series distributed by Spirit 2000, Inc.

Lipton, B. *The Biology of Belief.* Mountain of Love/ Elite Books, Santa Rosa, California, 2005.

Mitchell, S. *Tao Te Ching, A New English Version.* Harper Collins Publishers, Inc., New York, New York, 1992.

Nerburn, K. *Make Me an Instrument of Your Peace.* HarperCollins Publishers, New York, New York, 1999.

Reynolds, M. *Earthship, Volume 1.* Solar Survival Press, Taos, New Mexico, 1993.

Roth, G. *Breaking Free From Compulsive Eating.* Penguin Press, New York, New York, 1984.

Roth, G. *When You Eat at the Refrigerator, Pull Up a Chair.* Hyperion, New York, New York, 1998.

Siegel, B. *Love, Medicine, and Miracles.* Harper and Row Publishers, New York, New York, 1986.

Siegel, B. *Peace, Love, and Healing.* Walker Publishing Company, New York, New York, 1990.

Siegel, B. *Prescriptions for Living.* Quill, New York, New York, 1998.

Siegel, B. *Help Me to Heal.* Hay House, Carlsbad, California, 2003.

Siegel, B. *365 Prescriptions for the Soul.* New World Library, Novato, California, 2004.

Steen, A. *Straw Bale House.* Chelsea Publishing Company, White River Junction, Vermont, 1994.

Taylor, P. *Border Healing Woman.* University of Texas Press, Austin, Texas, 1981.

Tolle, E. *A New Earth.* Dutton, New York, New York, 2005.

Yogananda, P. *Where There is Light.* Self-Realization Fellowship, Los Angeles, California, 1988.

Yogananda, P. *The Essence of Self-Realization.* Crystal Clarity Publishers, Nevada City, California, 1990.

Yogananda, P. *In the Sanctuary of the Soul.* Self-Realization Fellowship, Los Angeles, California, 1998.